AF608378

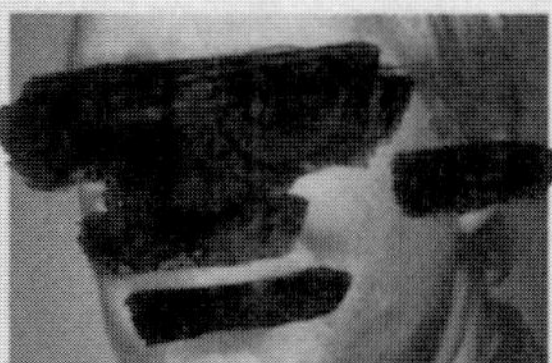

He's you're not responds, page 6

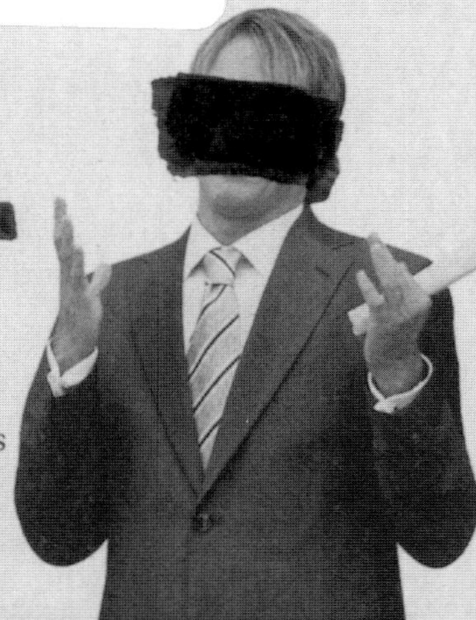

child's dad page 20

PAGE 6 15 27 32 59 85 92

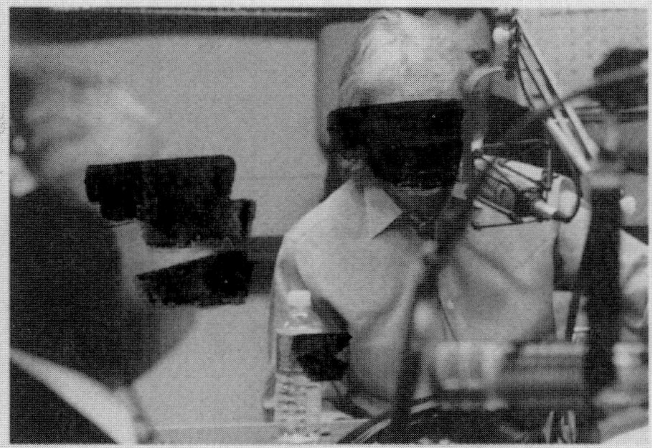

On the trail (with , page 32

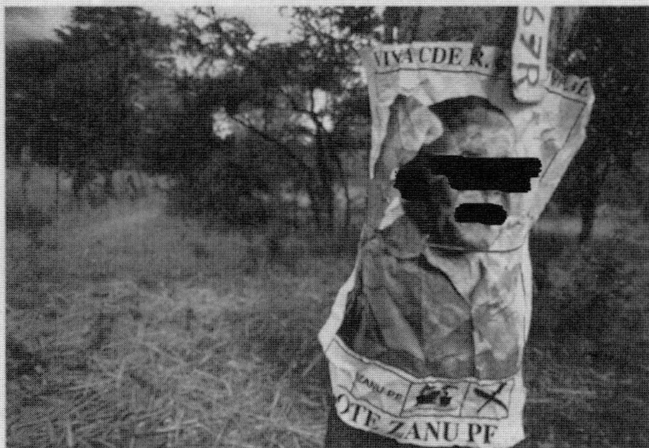

His image haun page 40

On the cover: Photo-Illustration. by Adhesive note from Insets, from left:

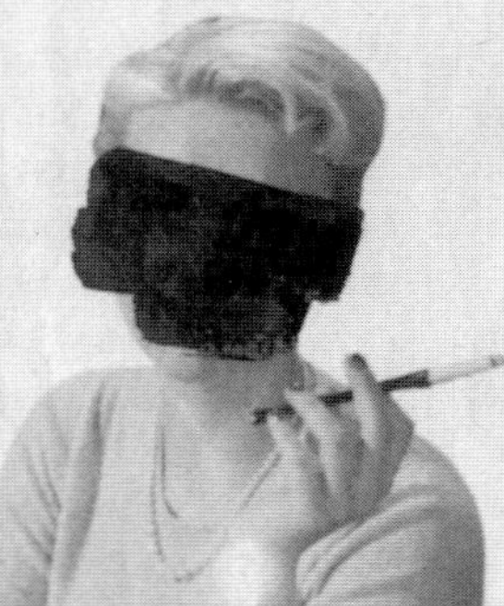

Butting in, page 59

ISBN 978-0-89439-028-9 DARK PROSPECTS by Charles Beronio is published by Printed Matter, Inc., 195 Tenth Avenue, New York NY 10011, USA, in February 2008. Printed Matter's Publishing Program for Emerging Artists is made possible through generous support from the Andy Warhol Foundation for the Visual Arts, the Foundation for Contemporary Arts, and through public funds from the New York State Council on the Arts, a state agency. For more information see www.printedmatter.org.

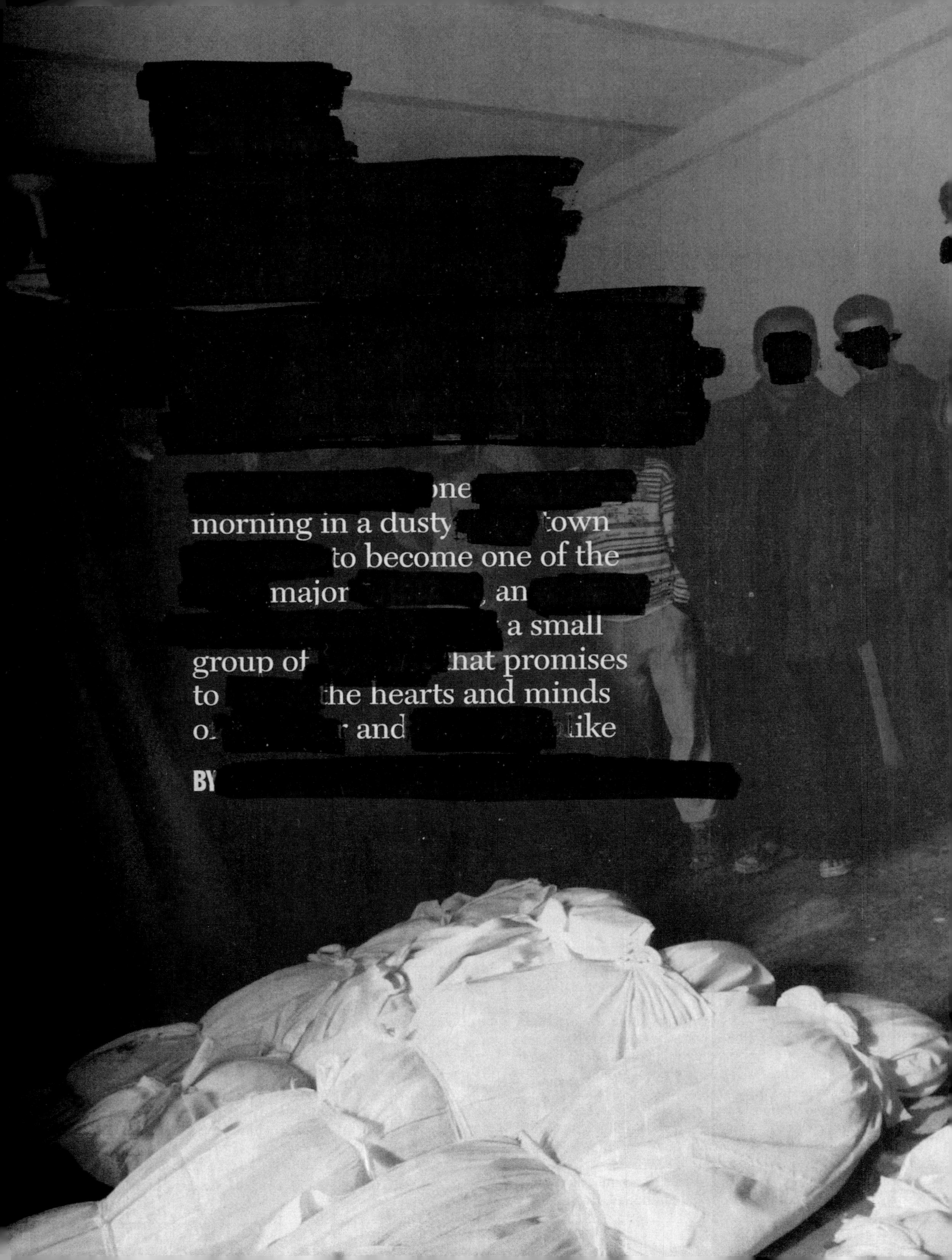

one
morning in a dusty town
to become one of the
major , an
a small
group of hat promises
to the hearts and minds
o r and like

BY

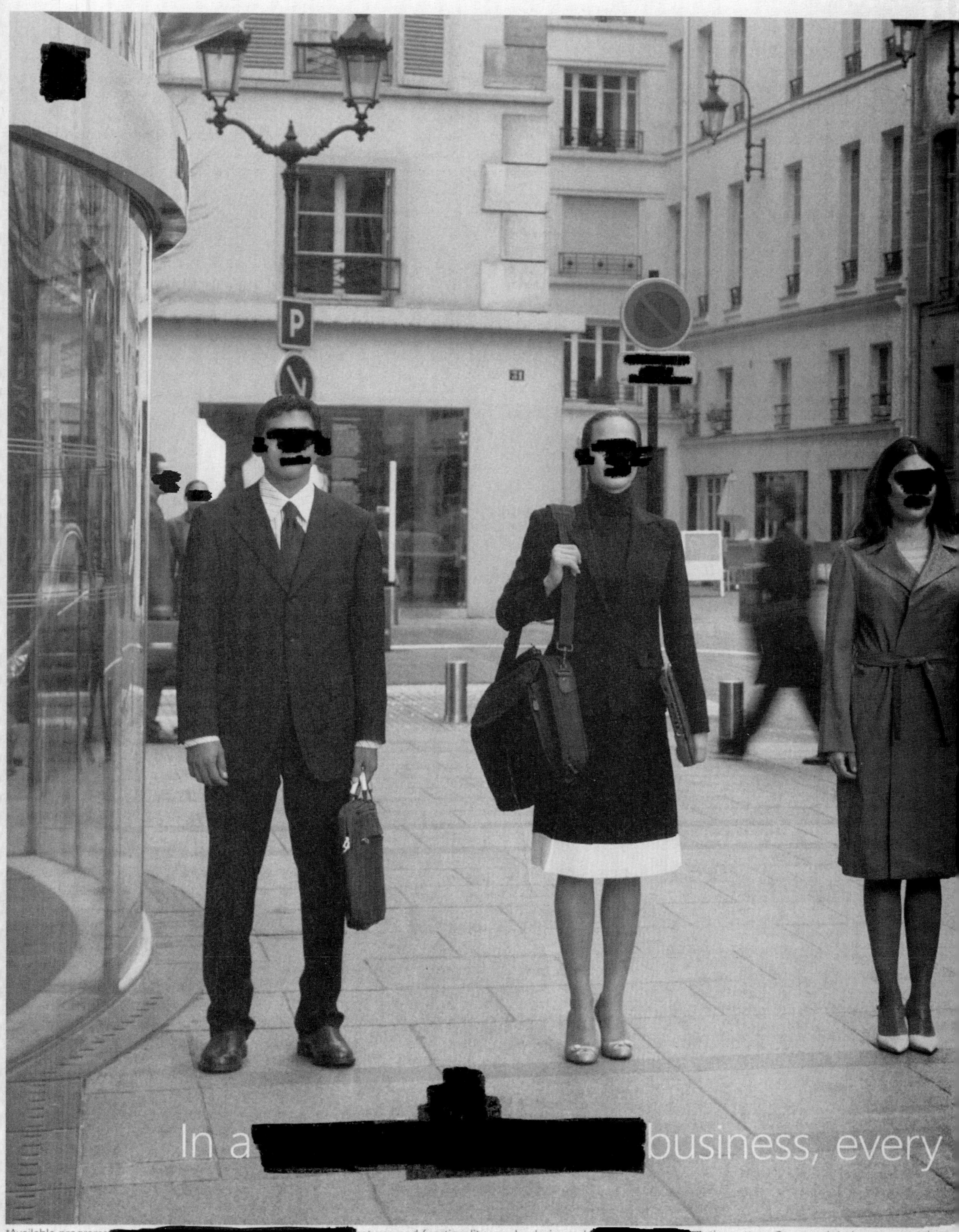

*Available programs eatures, and functionality vary by device and rating system. Connected devices, connectivity and over-the-air synchronization solutions may require separately purchased equipment and/or other wireless products (e.g., rd, network software, server hardware, or redirecto

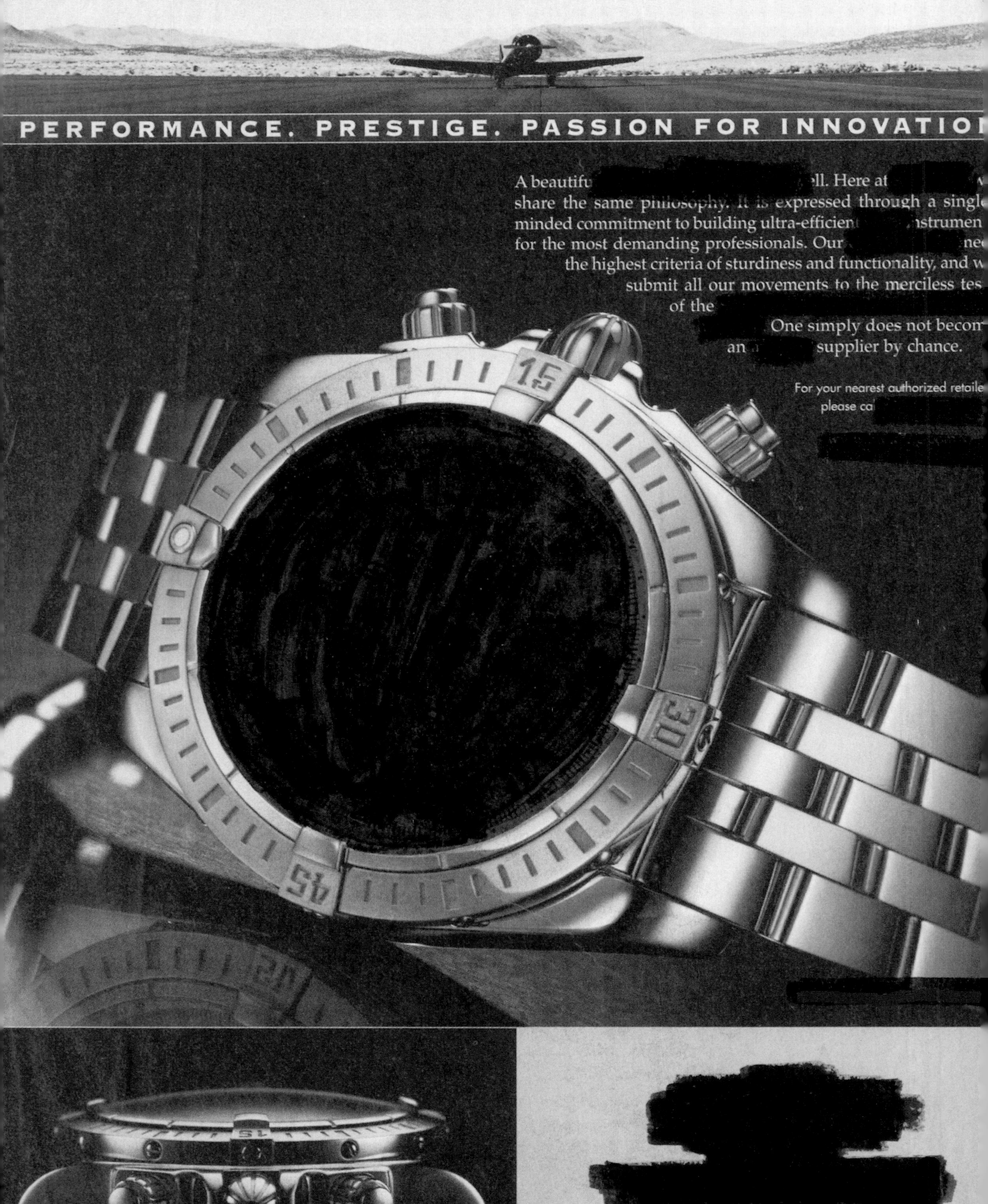
PERFORMANCE. PRESTIGE. PASSION FOR INNOVATIO
A beautifu ell. Here at
share the same philosophy. It is expressed through a singl
minded commitment to building ultra-efficient nstrumen
for the most demanding professionals. Our ne
the highest criteria of sturdiness and functionality, and w
submit all our movements to the merciless tes
of the
One simply does not becom
an supplier by chance.
For your nearest authorized retaile
please ca
15
30
45

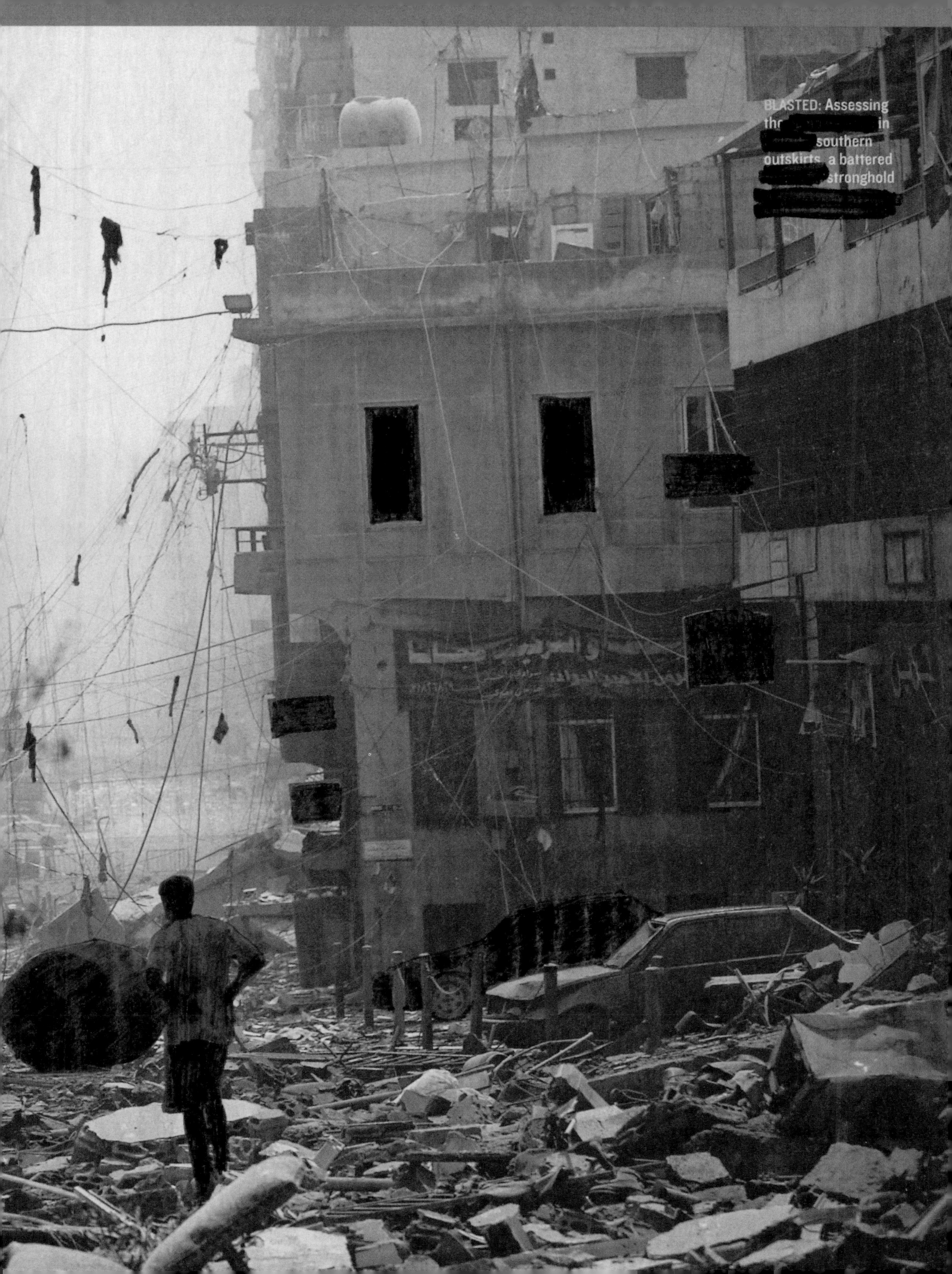

BLASTED: Assessing th[illegible] in [illegible] southern outskirts, a battered [illegible] stronghold [illegible]

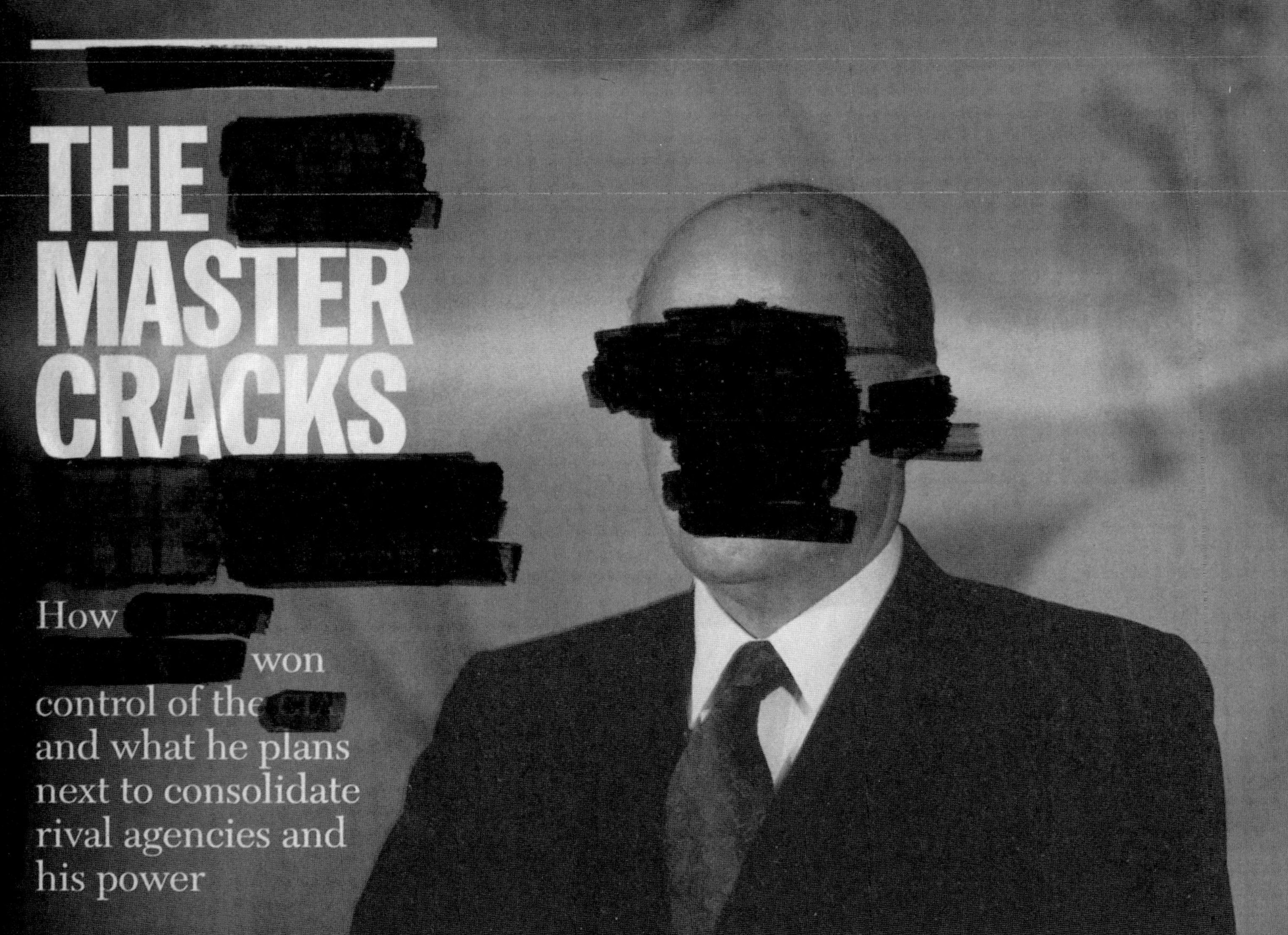

THE [illegible] MASTER CRACKS [illegible]

How [illegible] won control of the [illegible] and what he plans next to consolidate rival agencies and his power

By [illegible] N

COVERT OPERATIONS RARELY COME off exactly as planned. But last week's coup at th[illegible] orches-trated by [illegible] fficials a[illegible] ent-only slightly awry—and only at the last moment [illegible] icials had hoped to take the weekend to quietly prepare for the surprise announcement tha[illegible] ould replace embattled [illegible] th the two appearing together at t[illegible] ly this week. B[illegible] former spook [illegible] o used to run covert operations in [illegible] wanted to control the chore-o[illegible] aid, "[illegible]."

So a few hours after tendering his resig-nation to [illegible] e chief of sta[illegible] ducted an unusu[illegible] fare-thee-well for reporters, a show of calm that was designed to convey continuity at an agency that has known nothing but tur-bulence for the past five years.

Because it had been rumored about for months, [illegible] departure was one of those [illegible] isodes that are more sudden than surprising. [illegible] was alarmed to discover, within a few months after tak-ing over, how hard the job was. He lost some fights with rival intelligence agencies, particularly at [illegible] wasn't a very good manager, and while he had been put in the job to assert control over [illegible] eerists, the flow of ex-perienced [illegible] ing for the exit on his watch was steady and worrisome.

But most of all, he had been hired as [illegible] f at the very moment the job began to lose its clout. Less than a year after [illegible] stepped into the [illegible] post, [illegible] named [illegible] ector of national in-telligence [illegible] gave him the authority to oversee and direc[illegible] elligence shops—among them, th[illegible] y and [illegible] med with new powers created by [illegible] was supposed to make the hide-bound agencies work together and share information, something they had largely failed to do befo[illegible] eparture was, above all, a signal that [illegible] was finally exercising his powers and try-ing to slip the stray agencies into harness.

The move was overdue [illegible] struggled in his first year as spy czar [illegible] many of the well-entrenched agencies re-fused to bend to his will. The [illegible] offi[illegible] felt the [illegible] slow to lend a hand whe[illegible] the [illegible] was setting up his office. The F[illegible] complained, as it often does, about bei[illegible] underbudgeted. And [illegible] ad y[illegible] to prove to skeptics [illegible] t h[illegible] could wrest control of the [illegible] sive intelligence assets from [illegible] put them in service not just for military commanders but also for the entire intelli-gence community.

Yet in recent weeks, [illegible] his deputy, the hard-charging [illegible] hav[illegible] driven deep into the [illegible] kyard, chew-ing up its closely guarded turf and trying to bring the agency under their grip. In [illegible] t it be known that his office would be taking over the critical job of terrorism analysis—connecting the dots in all the raw data gathered on terrorists—a role th[illegible] had jealously guarded for decades. In an [illegible] usual public spee[illegible] likened th[illegible] o-change attitude about roles an[illegible]

There are other [illegible] almost kind of like it.

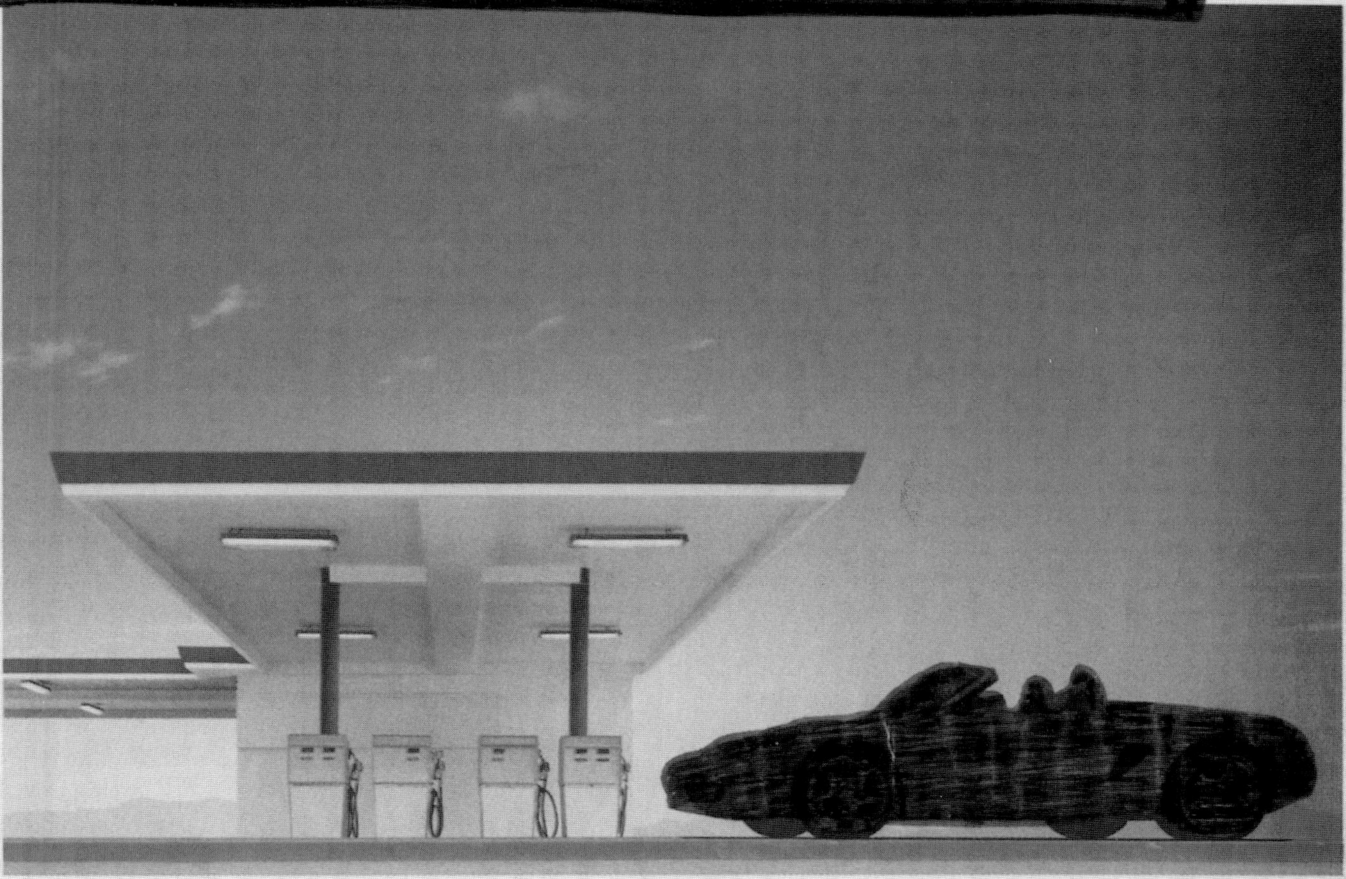

In an instant, thoughts of all else fall away. This is what [illegible] was meant to be [illegible] engine. Perfec[illegible] xact[illegible] race-bred chassis winding along blissfully twisting roads. In the open air, the sweet hum of its flat six tells you this is the on[illegible] There is n[illegible]

The [illegible] Starting at [illegible]

Isn't it time you had a of your own?

There are times in life when you could really use expert financial advice. For more than and its products have quietly earned a most enviable reputation. Visit for more information.

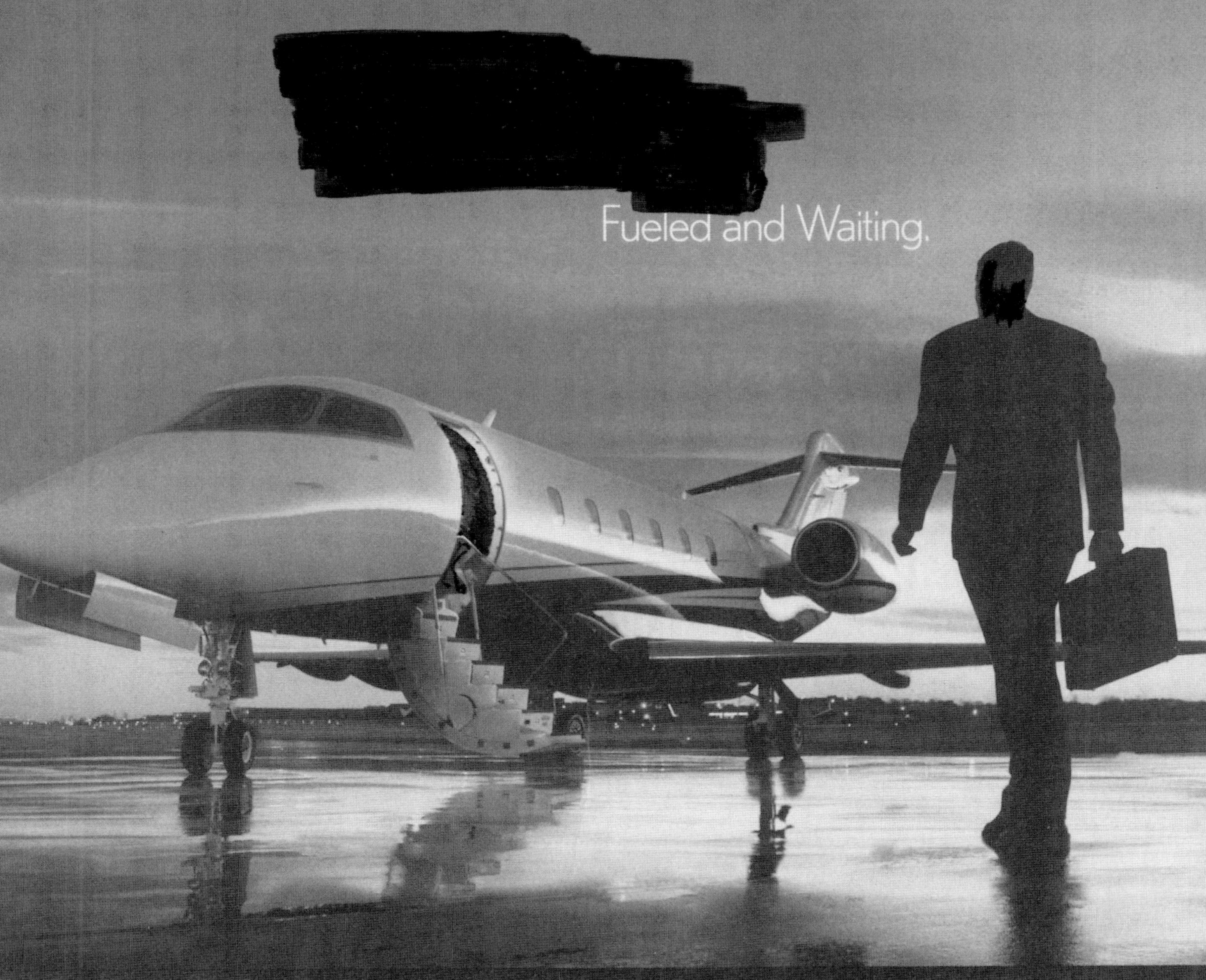
Fueled and Waiting.

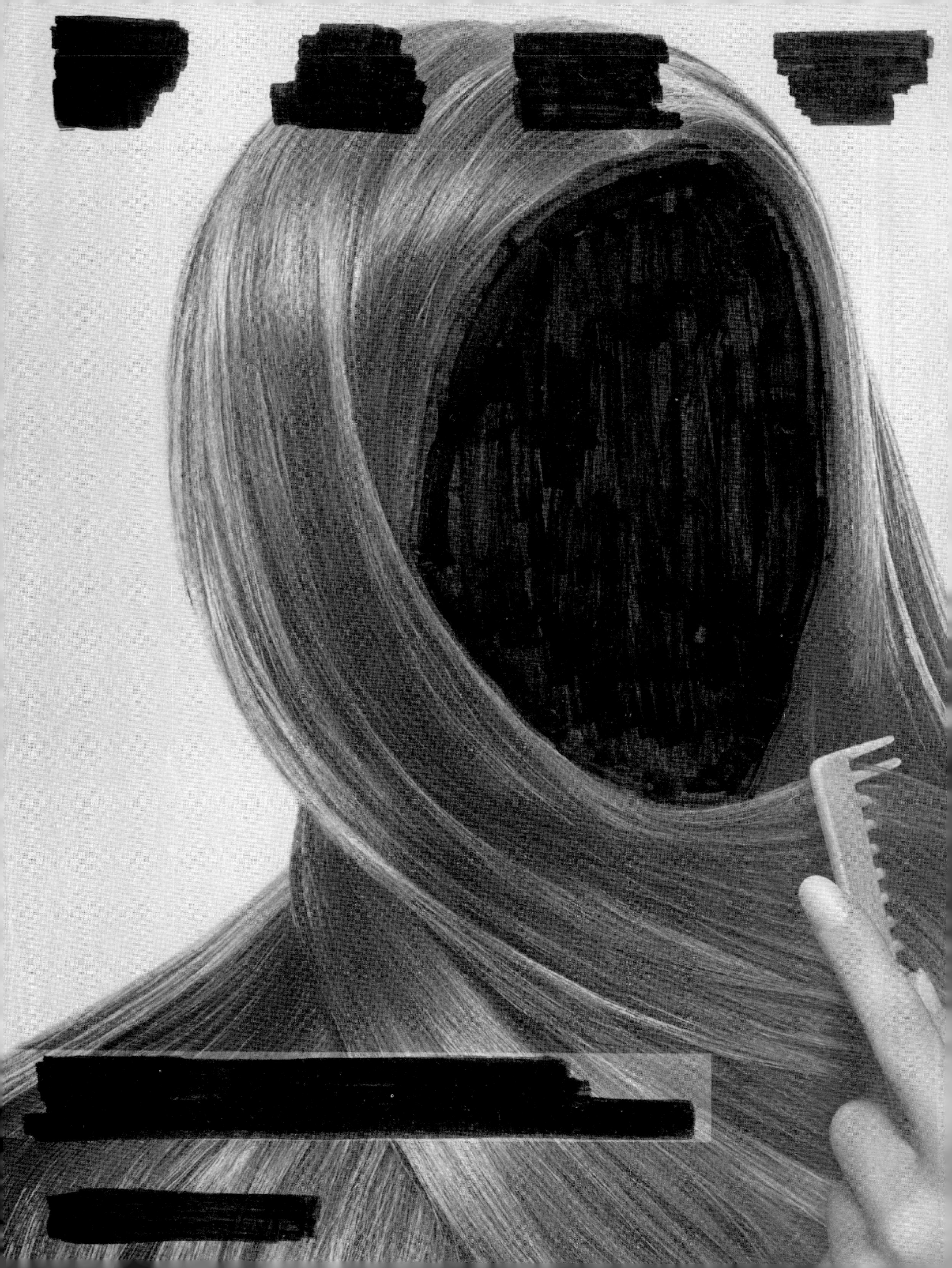

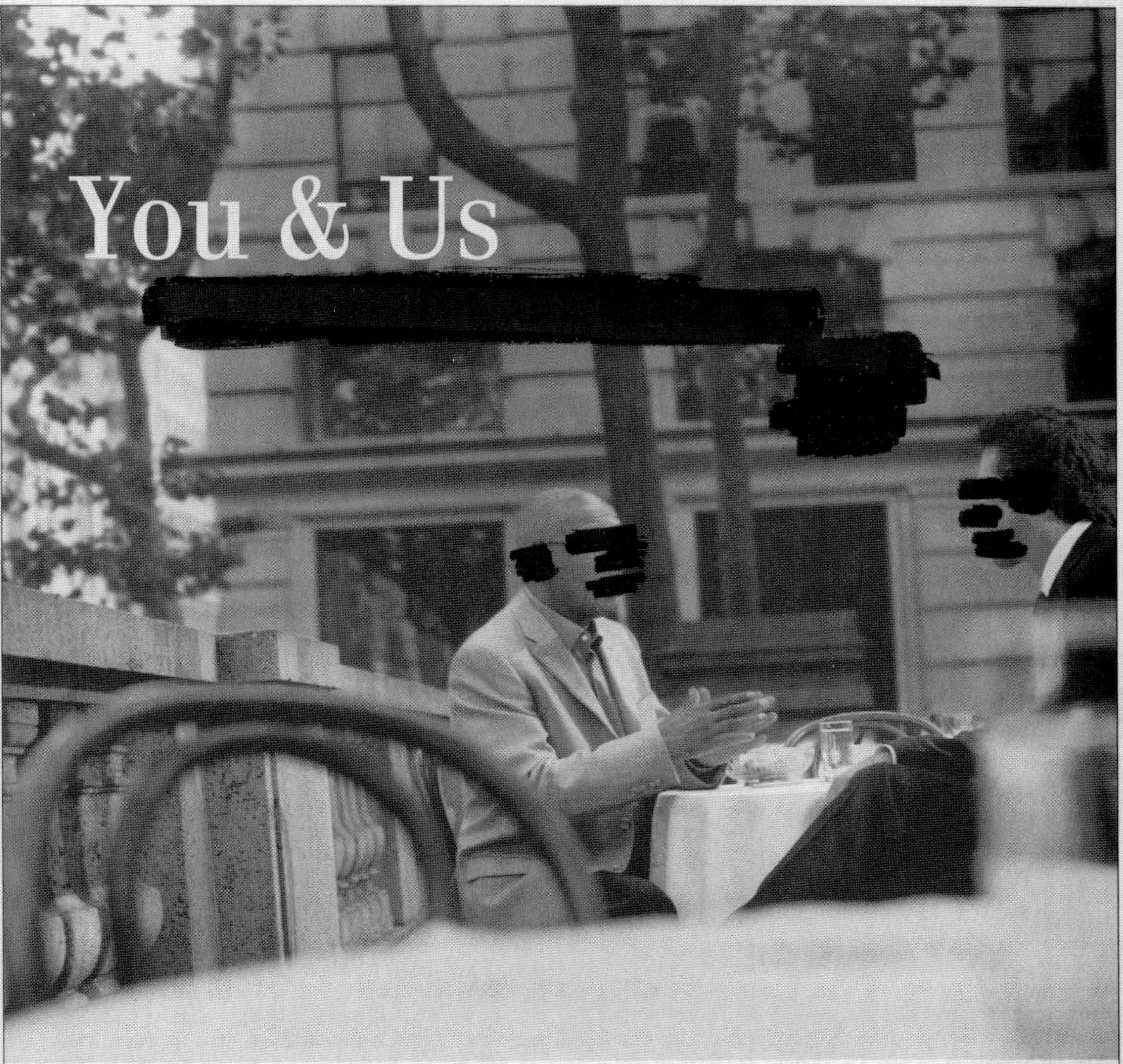

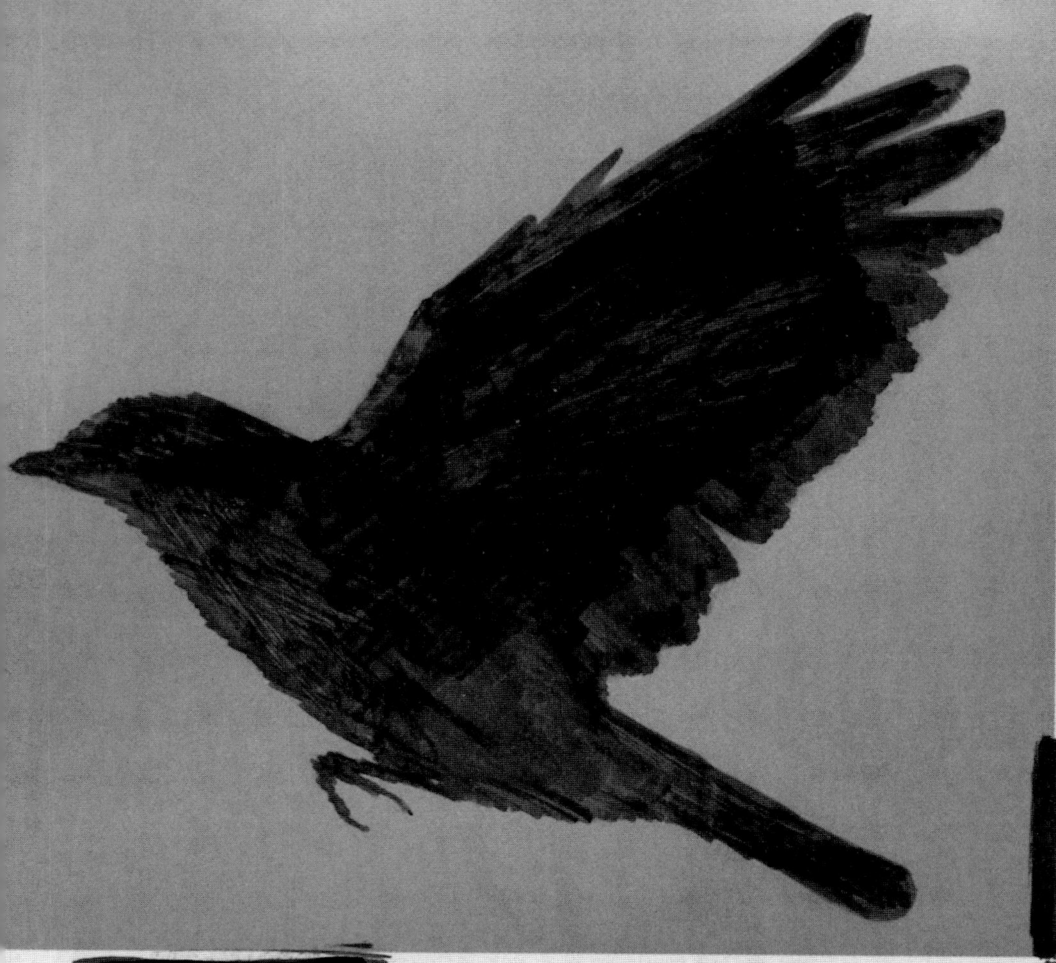

▲

PROBLEM **Climate change has shifted the peak season for the caterpillars it relies on to feed its hatchlings. By the time it arrives in some nesting grounds in the the food supply is already scarce**

winter in and return to their nesting grounds in the spring to lay eggs. When their hatchlings emerge, the parents feed them mostly with caterpillars. The timing of the flycatchers' migration has evolved over many thousands of years to coincide with an approximately three-week period afte plants have flowered and caterpillars are most abundant.

Thanks to warmer average temperatures, however, plants in some parts of the are flowering an average of 16 days earlier in the spring. The birds in don't know that; they still leave more or less at the usual time. And while the early spring they encounter in the north has induced them to move up egg laying a bit, they're still producing offspring nearly a week behind prime caterpillar season. Inadequate nourishment means dying birds and falling populations. "We think this is the first time anyone has really shown that an insufficient response to climate change can cause population declines," says study co-autho

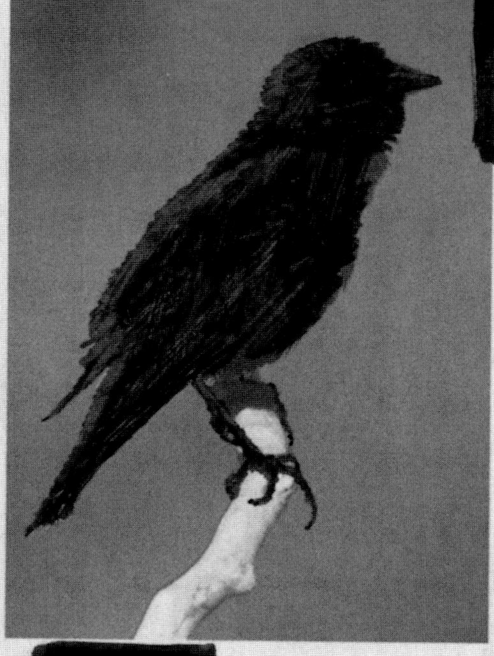

▲

PROBLEM **The tall grasses it needs for nesting are being developed for subdivisions or intensive farming; in some areas, it feeds in wetlands, which are also disappearing**

of the

But it's probably not the last warming might explain some migratory bird declines in as well, although director of bird conservation at the warns that it is dangerous to make assumptions.

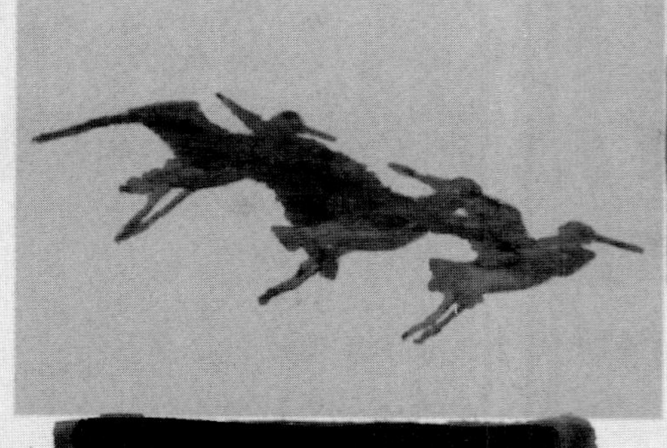

▲

PROBLEM **Wetlands where it breeds are vanishing because of changing rainfall patterns —possibly due to global warming—resulting in sharp population declines in some areas**

"It's great," he says, "when you have a bird like the er, which has been studied for you have enough detail to pinpoint what the problem is." The populations of some seabirds, such as are plunging not because the birds are having trouble timing their food supply but because the fish they feed on have shifted locations.

Other birds seem to be in trouble because of habitat loss. The decline of the rusty blackbird, for example—one of the most rapidly dwindling species in say may also be due to global warming, but the immediate cause seems to be a drying up of the wetlands where it breeds. The same may apply to the warbler. The also in decline, is losing use of global warming but because of another human activity: the destruction of mountaintop forests by coal operations.

And some birds are actually doing fine, adjusting to change and even increasing their numbers—at least in the bird counts. Some hummingbirds, for example, that used to winter i on't bother to make the trip anymore because now warm enough all year long. A number of migratory species that nest forests have rebounded because that part of the country is reforesting as agriculture declines are thriving, says because bluebird lovers have been setting up nesting boxes for them for the past half-century.

But even those success stories can be troubling. Natural ecosystems evolved at a glacial pace, over millenniums. And while human-induced change may help some species thrive, it can also throw off the balance that keeps an ecosystem healthy—as some hun hatchlings have discovered

LOVE TRIANGLE

The storied skyline gets a surge of exhilaration with the first worthy addition of the century

By

IF YOU LIKE TURMOIL THE PLACE to be right now. The had something like a prevailing style was in the at what appeared to be the tail end of Modernism. It was a moment when everybody knew the formula for a successful building—Glass + Steel = Box—and everybody was

We live now in a creative free-for-all, when Deconstruction, Expressionism and a half a dozen other unorthodoxies reign. But as it turns ou er actually died. What it did was imes into something really interesting. To see what that means stand and run your eyes up and silhouette of building by the r. What you'll be looking at may be the most gratifying specimen of since office dropped on o years ago. Or maybe since his transparent dome for the Or his serene and lucid courtyard You get the picture.

his first sizable project in the rises from within brown masonry base that dates from the t's when news-

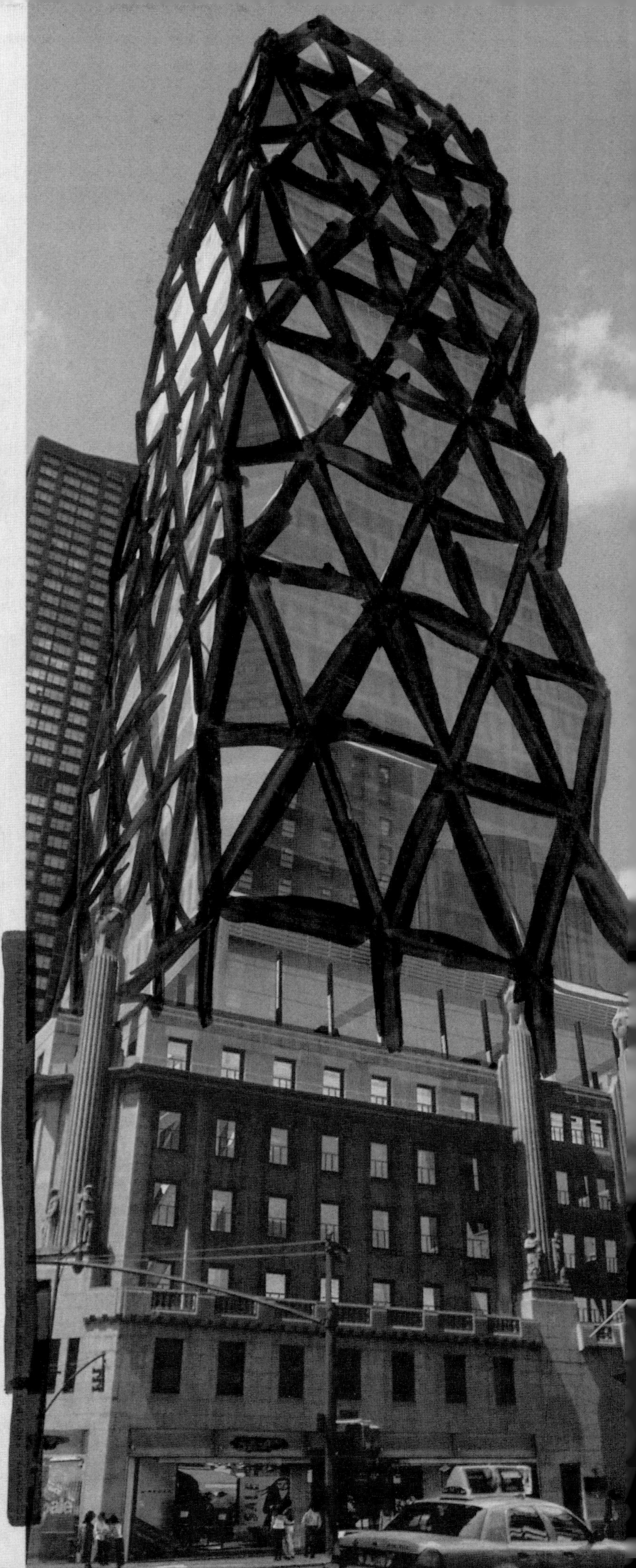

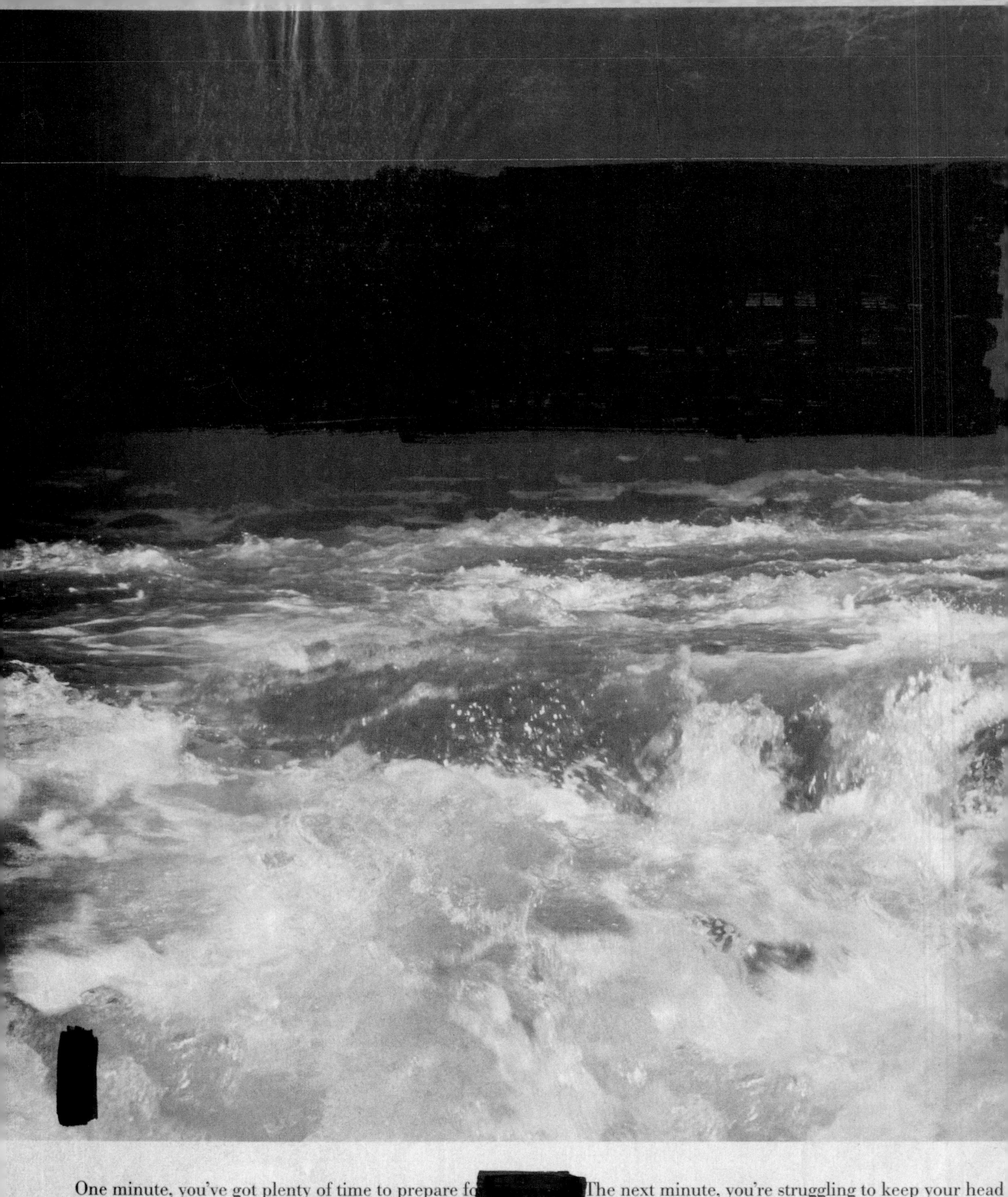

One minute, you've got plenty of time to prepare fo[redacted] The next minute, you're struggling to keep your head above water. Fortunatel[redacted] has made[redacted] a whole lot easier. Just stop by one of our neighborhood offices, where a[redacted] will meet with you face-to-face to get to know your unique needs better. And to help you achieve you[redacted], we'll recommend[redacted] that have proven

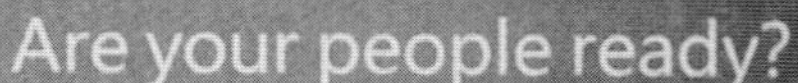

They're your biggest competitive advantage, but only if you give them the right tools. Like software that streamlines the busywork, serves up the right information, and helps integrate the whole company. Software that makes people ready, so they can make all the differenc

Software for the

In a business,

there's a secret weapon in every swivel chair.

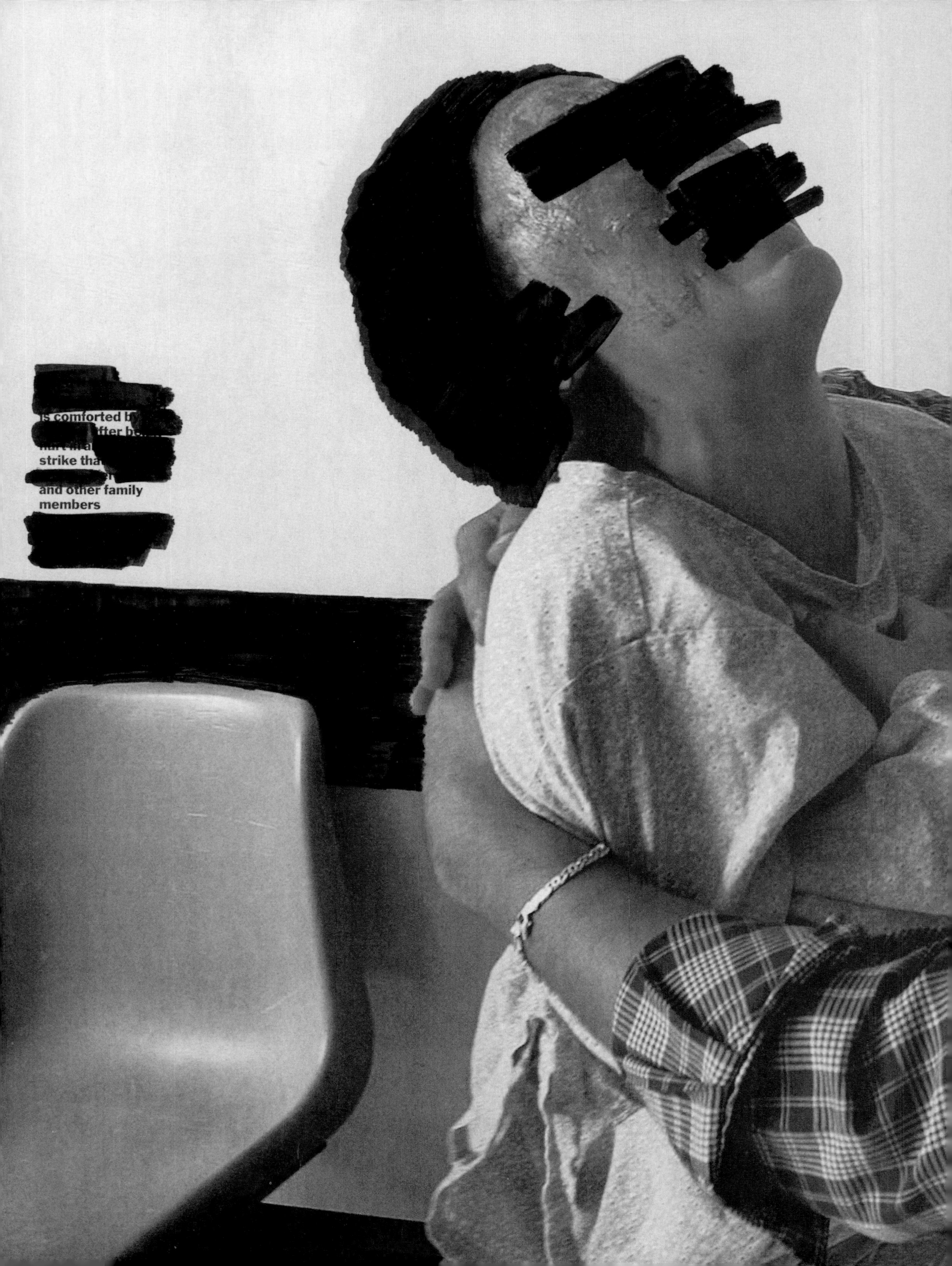
is comforted
strike
and other family
members

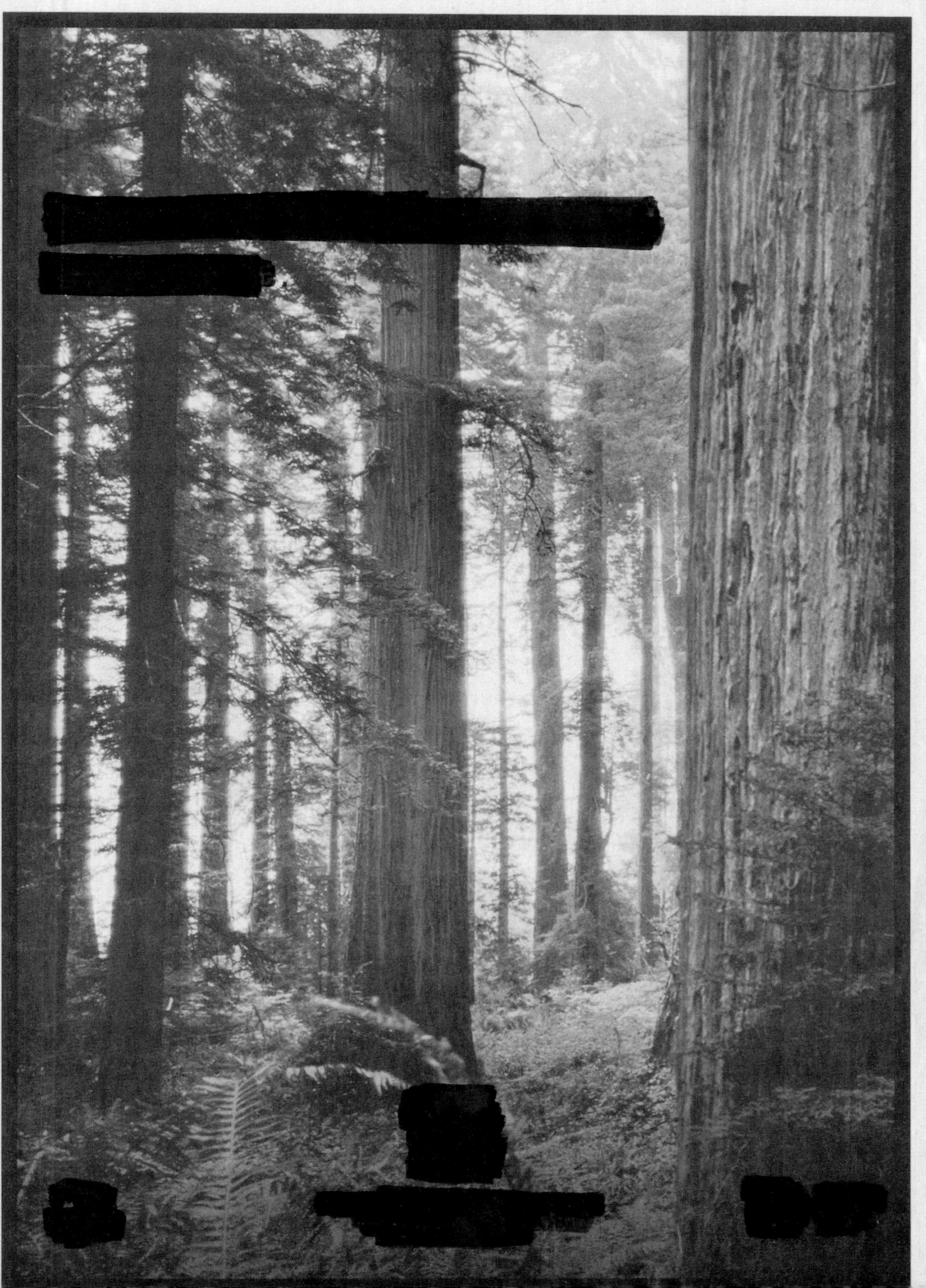

has rubbed off on hawks like the primary in- policies. "There's a toward th proach of focusing entirely on vital interests," says a presidential adviser.

To much of the world, that's a relief. But having expended so much energy and so many resources o nd the war in th is

are witnessing an overhaul of the old Doctrine, but the question is, Can the find a new one to take its place?

■ THE EFFECT

IT MAY BE TOO SOON TO SAY WHETHER HISTORY will l s decision to invade nd his aides insist will happen. But the very fact that parts ain on the edge of chaos after three years of and the deaths of more than incontrovertible evidence of how the

retire who commanded th from 199 to Now we Meanwhile, to take.

Fighting the insurgency in eroded the appeal of th in a more mundane but way: it's exhausting. Public backing for the war rose slightly after the killing of terrorist leader in month, but the unremitting body count has pushed those numbers back down again. More than half the public believes going to war was not worth the cost. The drain on resources is becoming embarrassing. According to the s, the diversion of money for partly responsible for a shortfall fund that has left one base, unable to buy office supplies. Another base has received utility disconnection notices.

There is another cost, and that is the drain of brainpower and psychic energy in th from th on down. Governments habitually overestimate what they can achieve and underestimate how much of their working day they have to spend on the really tricky issue at hand. say he and they can multitask— ," says one—but the ceaseless need to make a bad situation passable is a drag on the entire enterprise.

STABILIZER with in th ffice last week, has led a shift toward realism

finding that other global challenges—from the turmoil in th to the genocide in the regional ambitions o ave grown beyond its ability to do anything about them. " official unde ." At the same time, there is a danger tha belated embrace of conventional diplomacy will turn out to be a cover for disengagement, at a time whe leadership is still required to fend off civil war i nd deter the ambitions o o say nothing o we

miscalculations have come back to haunt it. Topplin was to be the singular demonstration of th quick and decisive strike against tyranny in the heart of the It would also send a message to the rest of the world's malefactors, including and , to think twice about testing the patience with regimes bent on acquiring weapons of mass destruction.

As it turns ou may prove to be not only the first but also the last laboratory for preventive war. Instead of deterring the rulers i and g, the travails of the occupation may have emboldened those regimes in their quest to obtain nuclear weapons while constraining th military's ability to deter them says

■ TWILIGHT OF IDEALISM

IF THE GRIND OF THE WAR I HAS undermined one plank of Doctrine—pre-emption—the complexity of global politics has caused the to struggle in its goal to spread democracy as a defense against terrorism. Some democracy activists give credit for giving a jump start to limited reforms in close regimes such as But the was premature, at best, in its hopes for dramatic change. In which th has praised in the past for opening its political process, the government o has launched a renewed crackdown against its political opponents. another onetime success story championed has witnessed an unraveling coalition of parties that led with-

The real international gold standard.

For over a century, the [redacted] name has stood for authentic, uncompromising quality. Prized by captains of industry, heads of state and the most successful independent pacesetters, a [redacted] has always been, and remains, the ultimate reward. With its elegantly appointed cabin and deep reserves of smooth power, the technologically advanced [redacted] offers a truly distinctive driving experience. Every element of this magnificent sedan is designed to achieve one goal: to make each moment spent behind the wheel an eagerly anticipated and long remembered event. We invite you to experience th[redacted] and discover for yourself why it just may be the real international gold standard.

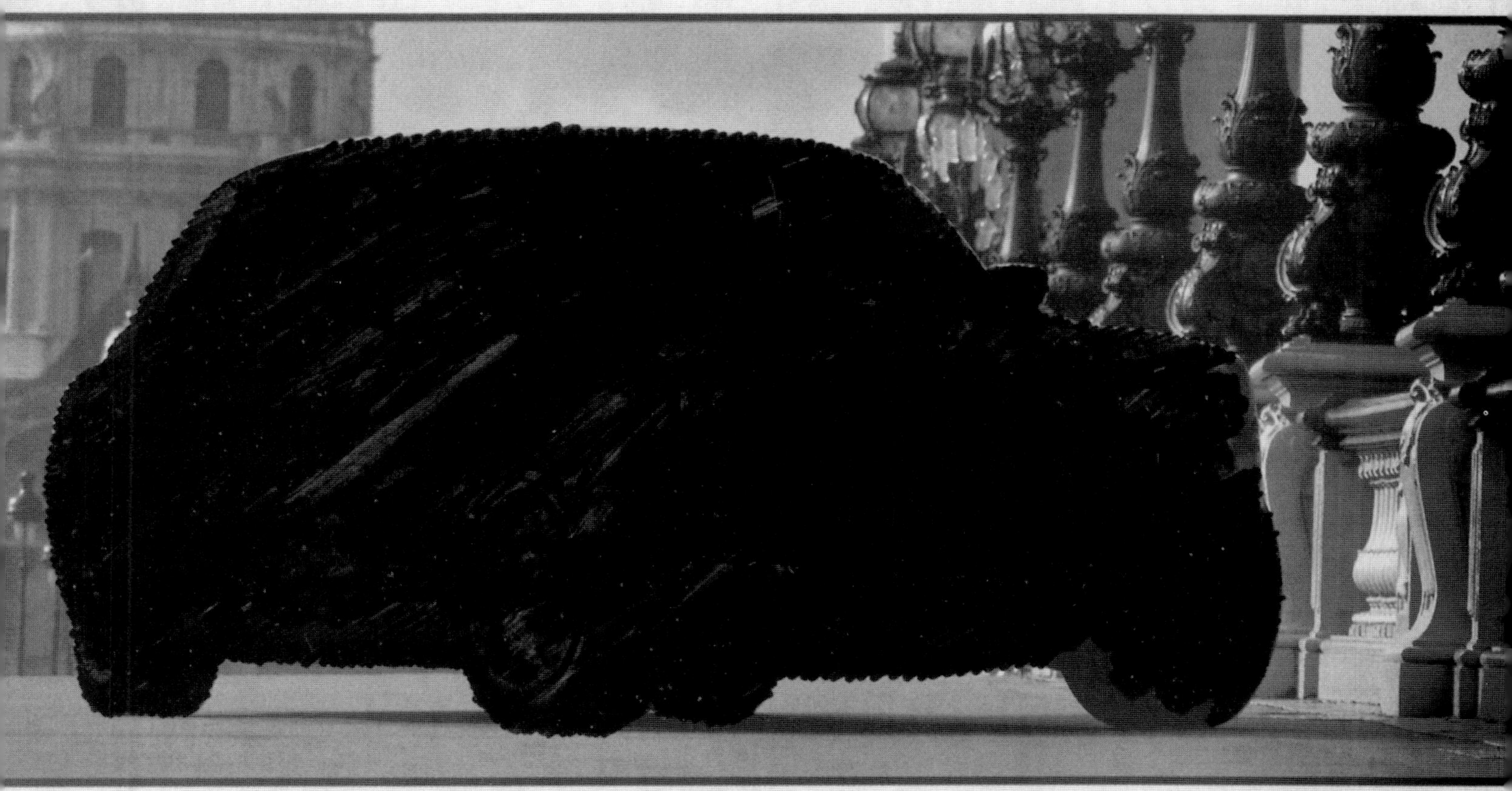

Visit your Authorized [redacted] aler in the following locations:

For more information, visi[redacted]m or cal[redacted]

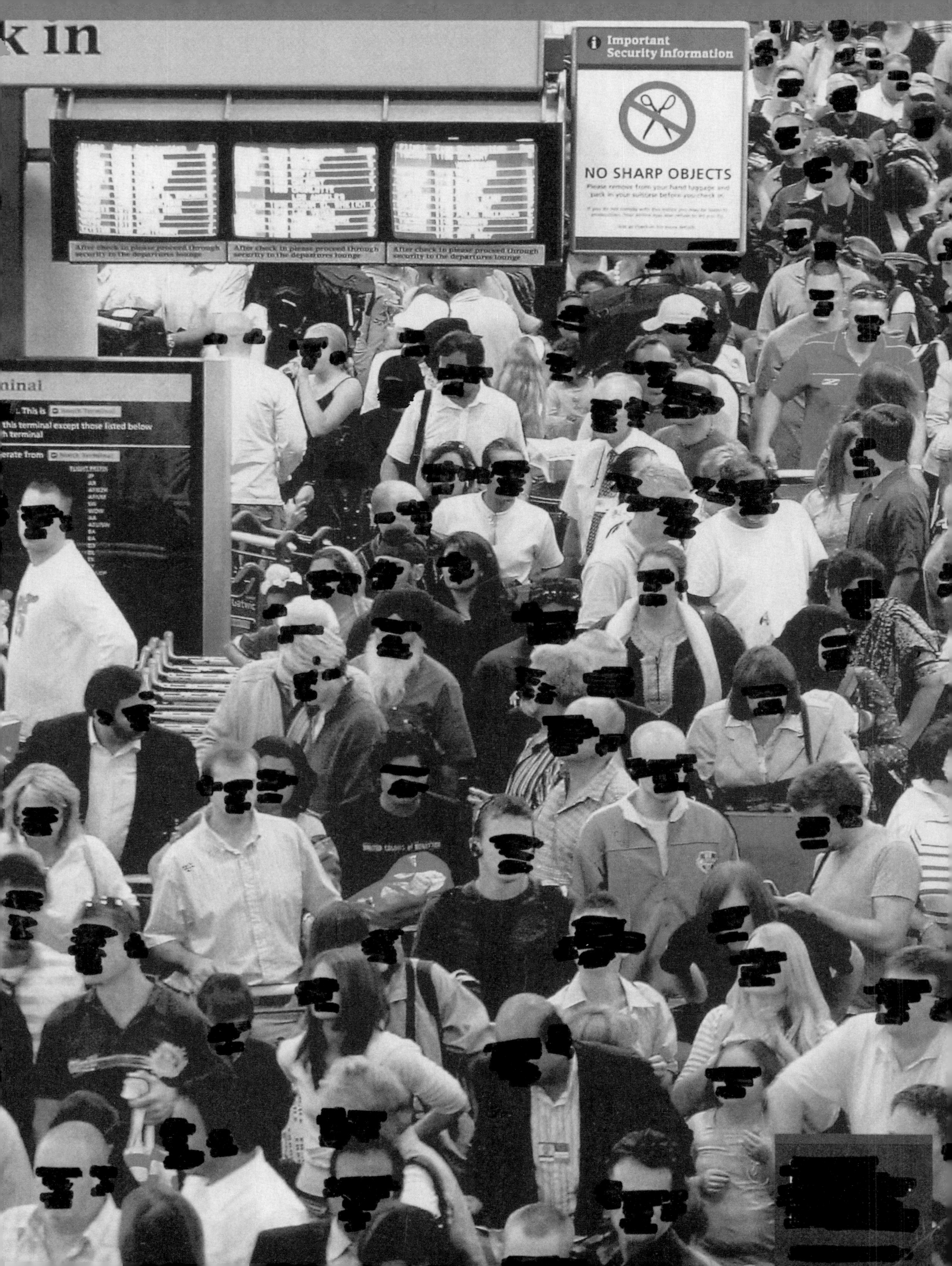
k in
Important
Security information
NO SHARP OBJECTS
Please remove from your hand luggage and
pack in your suitcase before you check in.
After check in please proceed through
security to the departures lounge
After check in please proceed through
security to the departures lounge
After check in please proceed through
security to the departures lounge
minal
. This is
this terminal except those listed below
h terminal
erate from

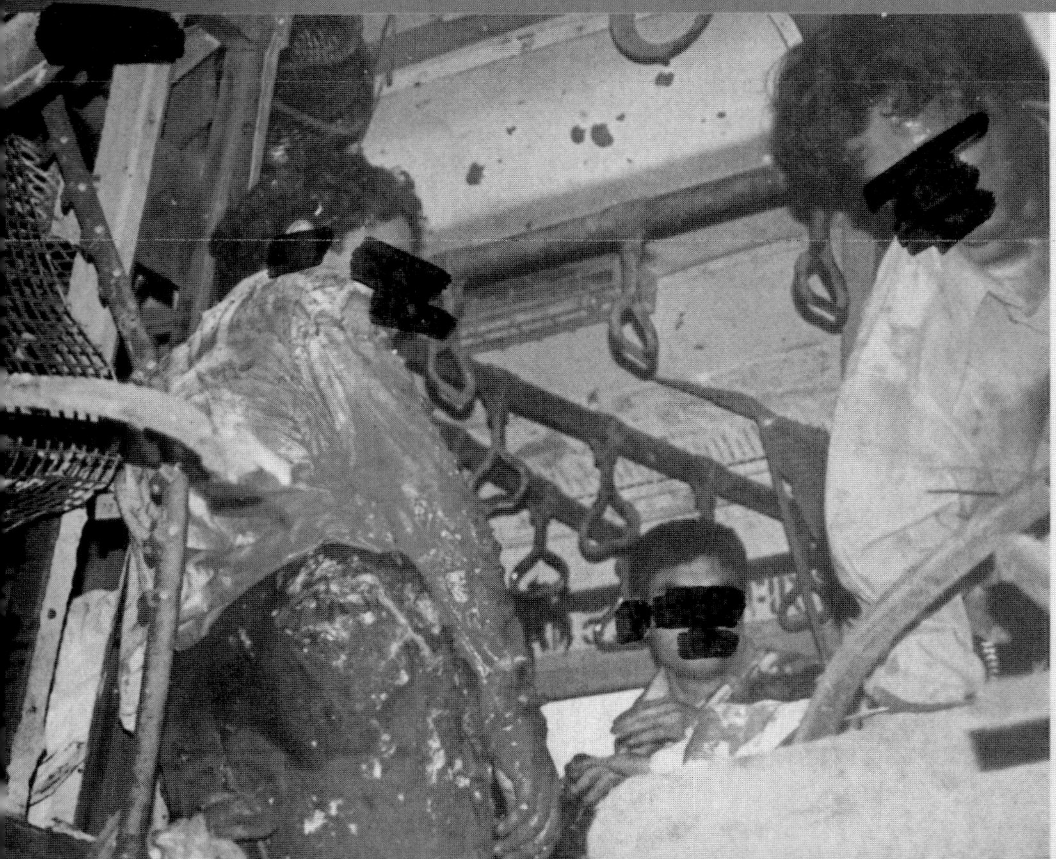

Terror on The Tracks

Worrisome suspects in [illegible] train bombings

BY [illegible]
AN[illegible]

THEY SEEM TO HAVE DRAWN little notice as they squeezed aboard the packed first-class carriages. Most passengers were concentrating on getting home from a long, rainy [illegible] at the office in [illegible] financial center, [illegible] The men placed their duffel bags and metal lunchboxes on the overhead luggage racks, and then, apparently, pushed their way off again, unnoticed—until [illegible] when the explosions began. Within [illegible] bombs had ripped through seven suburb-bound commuter trains on the same rail line. The blasts left [illegible] and [illegible] dead or dying and nearly [illegible]ured in the wreckage.

Police investigators are increasingly convinced they know who was behind the [illegible] style bombings. Only two terrorist organizations in the region have the skills and resources for such a massive, coordinated attack—and this, police believe, was a joint operation by both networks. One alleged partner is [illegible], a [illegible] separatist group that has been outlawed since [illegible] n [illegible] the country where it began [illegible] ago. The other group is the banned [illegible], a homegrown jihadist outfit that is spreading rapidly among disaffected young [illegible] across much of [illegible] Both groups are denying any involvement, but police say evidence against them is piling up.

THE AFTERMATH: Carnage inside [illegible] station moments after the blasts (top), what's left of a train car (above), an injured commuter waiting for family

The authorities released photos of three bearded young men in connection with the attacks. Police identified one of them as the fugitive ringleader of a dozen alleged [illegible] operatives who were arrested two months ago in [illegible] some [illegible] miles east of [illegible]. In the course of that sweep, police seized dozens of [illegible] automatic rifles, crates of ammunition and more than [illegible] pounds of military-grade plastic explosive. The arrests had resulted from an investigation that began earlier this year after cops apprehended a pair of suspected [illegible] operatives getting off a train in downtown [illegible]. Police say the men had two pounds of plastic explosive in their possession.

The two organizations are united by the same wild-eyed cause: a dream of bringing the entire [illegible] back under [illegible] rule for the first time since the [illegible]. As followers of a harshly intolerant strain of [illegible] they reject any notion of majority rule in a land where [illegible] outnumber [illegible] partnership has been growing for several years, and in the past year or so [illegible] police believe that the two groups have collaborated on a series of attacks, including the bombing of a temple this [illegible] in [illegible] holiest city, [illegible] and the [illegible] bombing of two [illegible] markets, killing more than [illegible]

The alliance makes both groups more dangerous than ever. Thousands of armed guerrillas are believed to have attended [illegible] training camps in [illegible] police think [illegible] may have [illegible] hard-core members and as many as [illegible] sympathizers who can be relied on for assistance and shelter. With [illegible] support, [illegible] fighters can now operate deep inside [illegible] without a lifeline to [illegible]istan's side of the border. That development has raised new fears of international terrorism on [illegible] soil. [illegible] to take advantage of [illegible] anger," warns [illegible] a former [illegible] has always denied any ties to [illegible]. But the echoes of [illegible] are deafening. ■

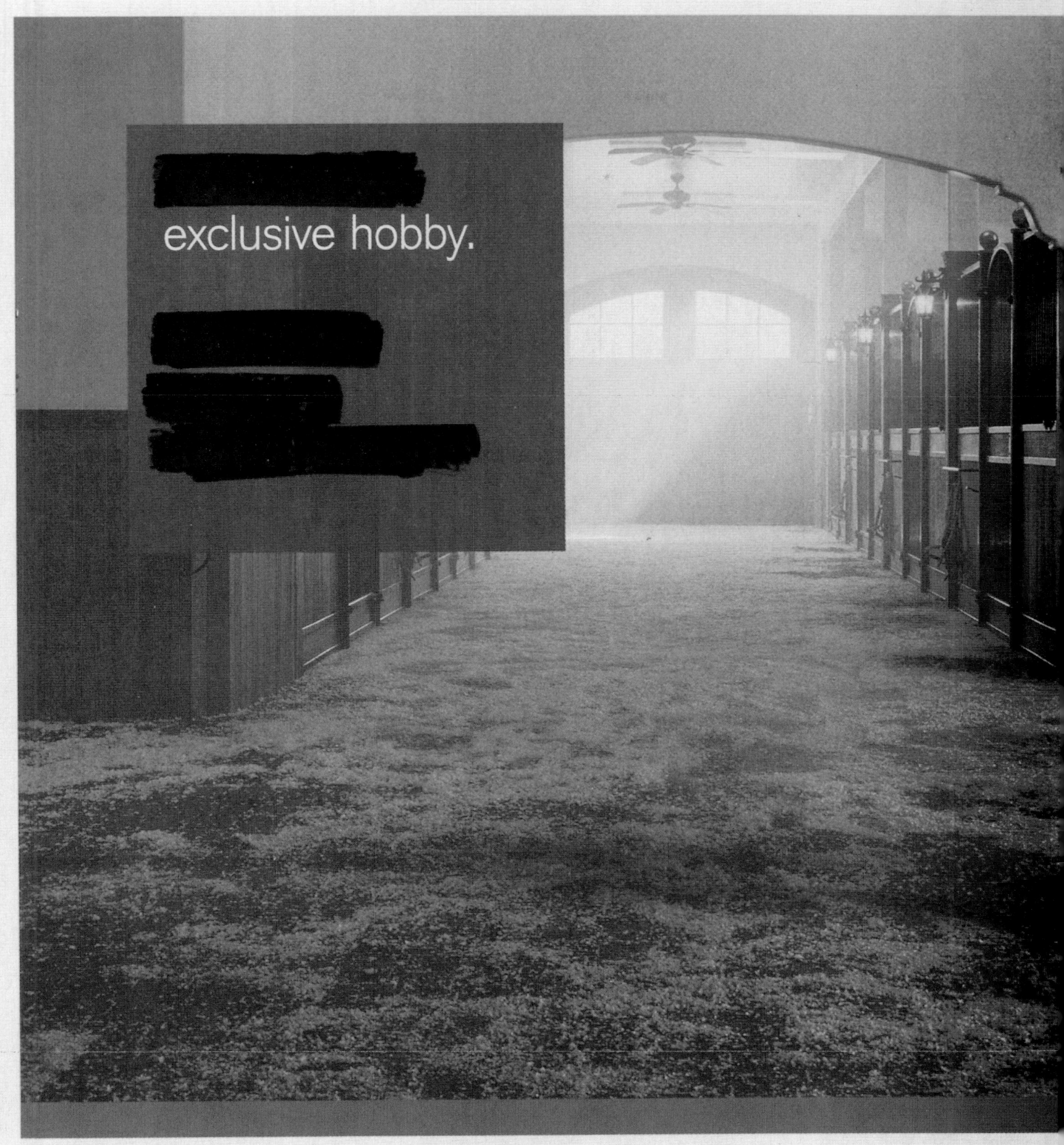

Since we have focused on bringing new perspectives to our clients. Understanding the past, but shaped by the future. Always looking at opportunities and challenges from a different point of view. Because we know what it takes to successfully maintain wealth. And to turn passionate work into great results.

ww

NOW TAKE 15% OFF
ONLINE SHIPMENTS.

WE KNOW WE HAD YOU AT

New and existing account holders can sav ist rates on eligibl shipments when using t fedex.com. Combined with convenient access to shipment processing, document preparation and a host of other online tools, you'll save both time and money. Go t or more information.

ited-time offer valid from through nly. Registered accounts will receiv r list rates online shipments made afte Restrictions may apply. See Program Agreement terms for details.

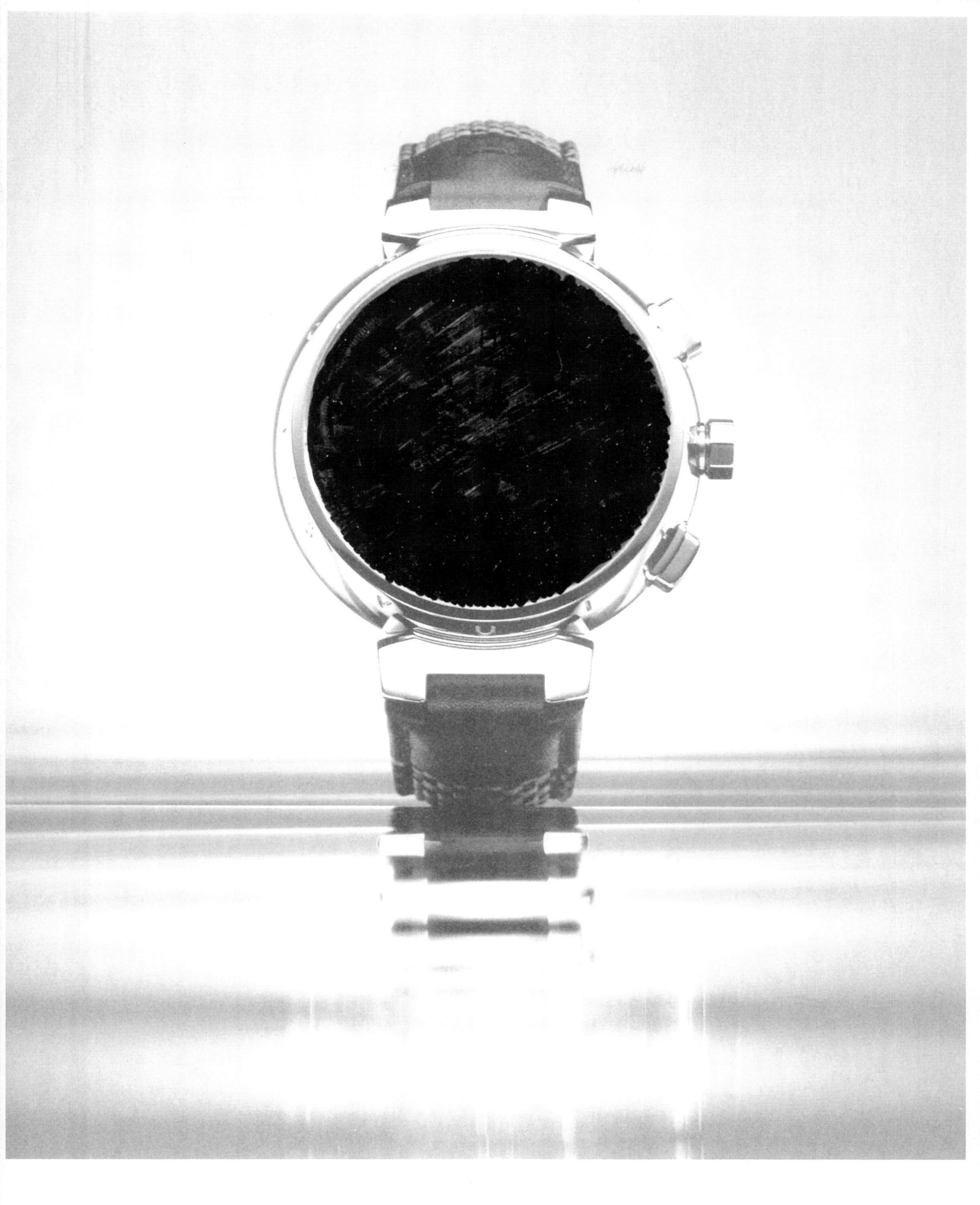

automatic chronograph. Countdown and fly back

Sold exclusively in

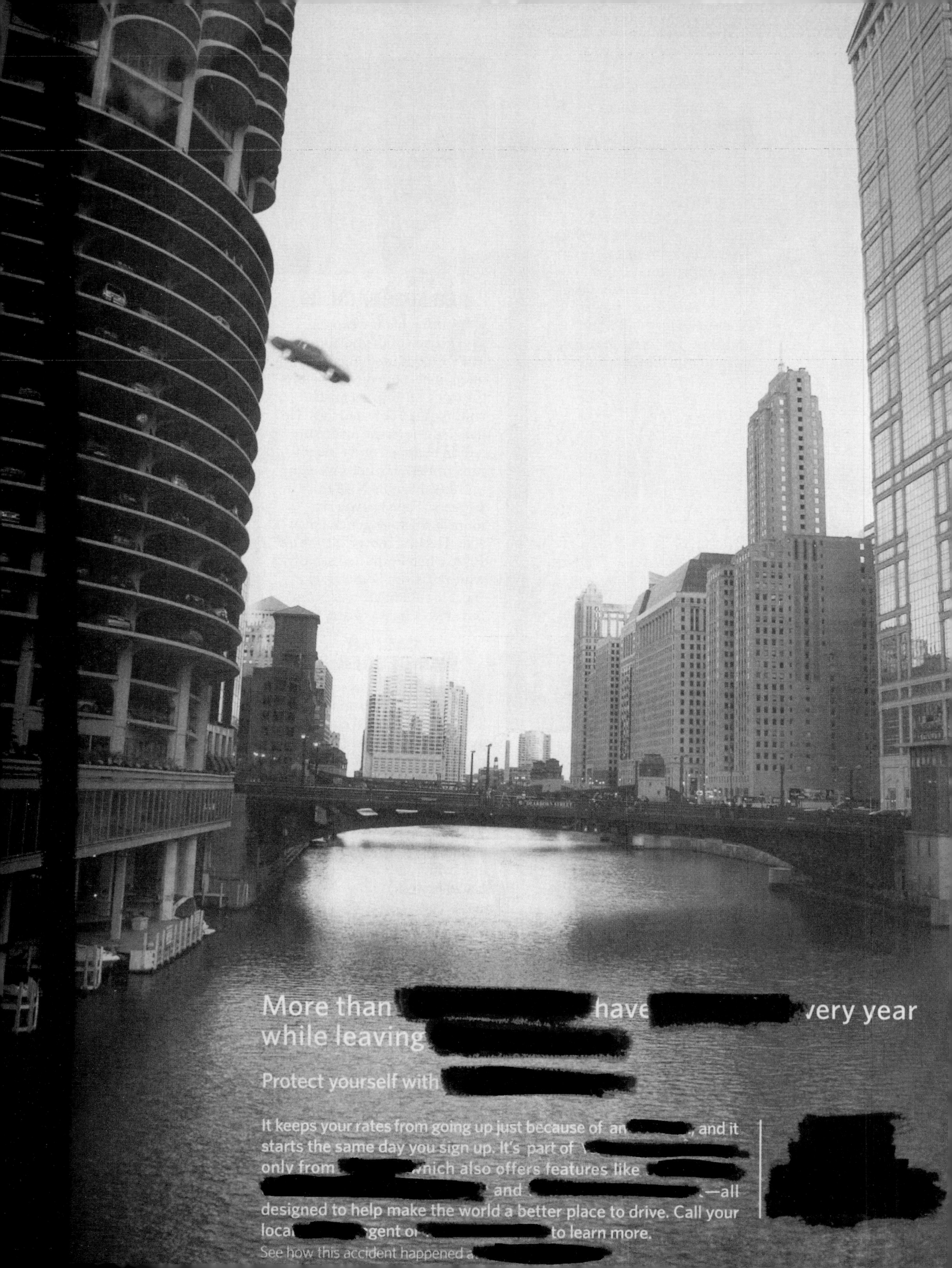
More than have very year
while leaving
Protect yourself with
It keeps your rates from going up just because of an , and it starts the same day you sign up. It's part of only from which also offers features like and —all designed to help make the world a better place to drive. Call your local agent or to learn more.
See how this accident happened a

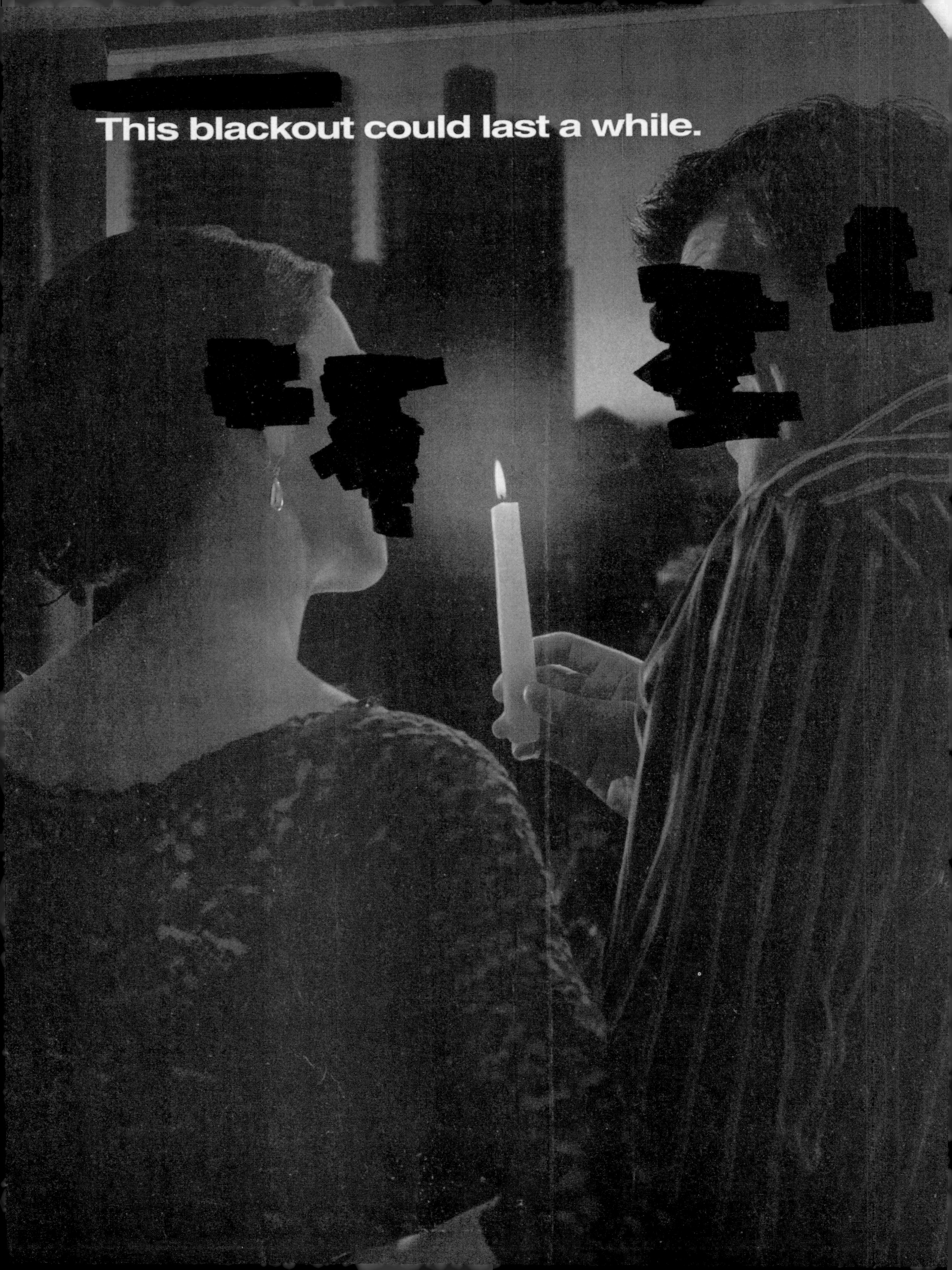
This blackout could last a while.

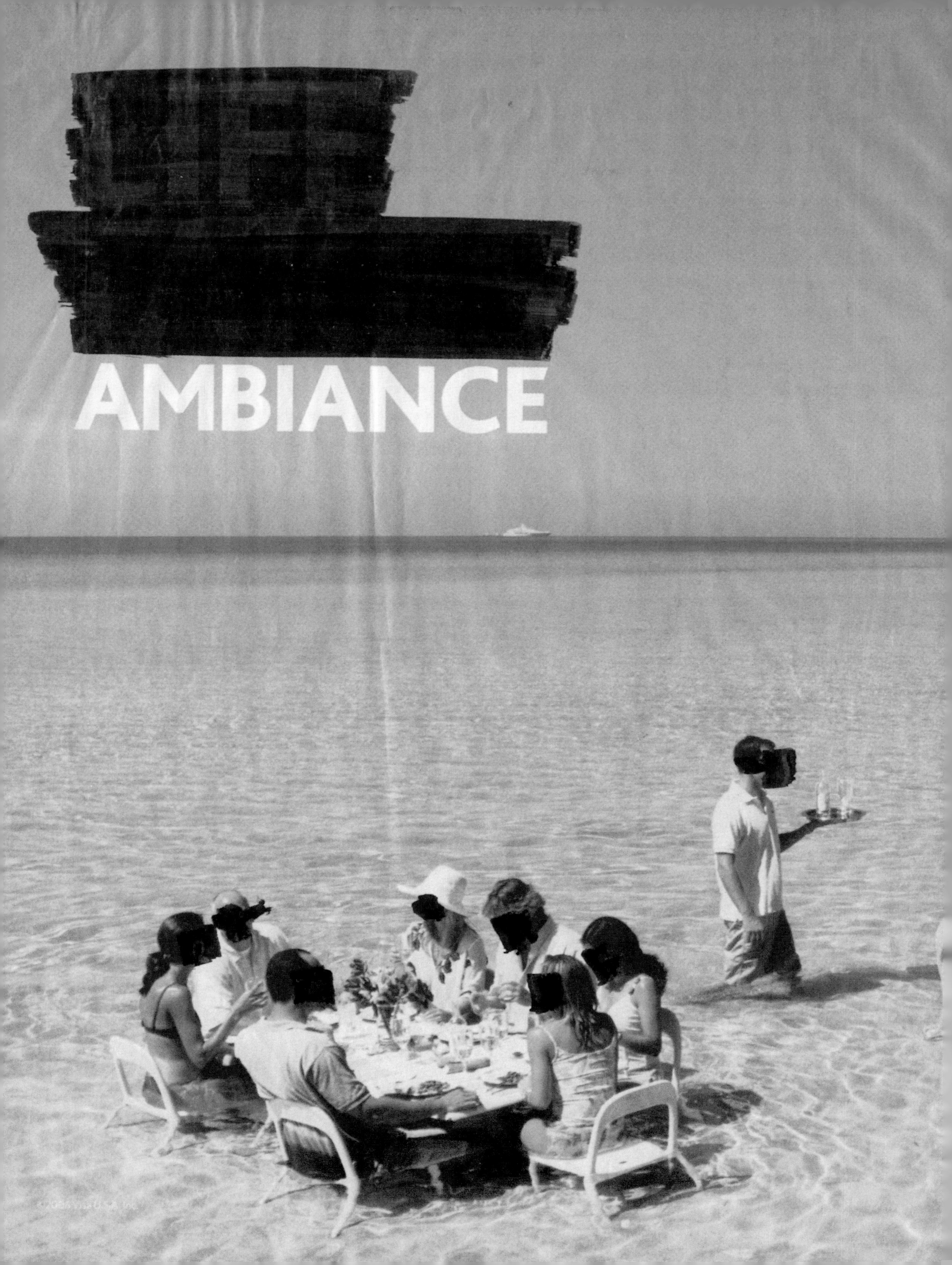

AMBIANCE

T THE

andled the bigges of term. A exclusive.

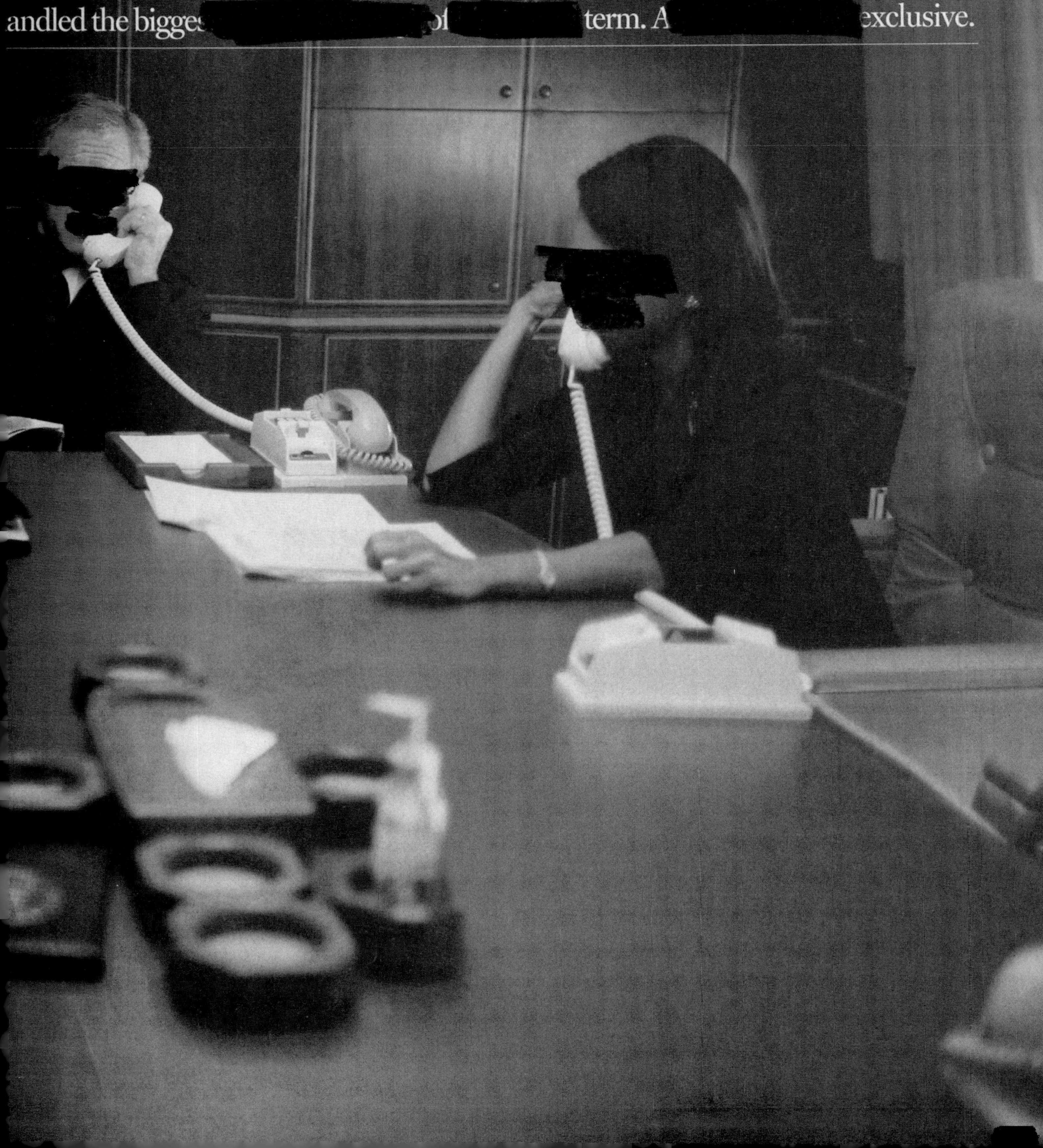

Stocks still low?

Invest now ooming real estate market.

nationally-recognized company dedicated to showing people like you how to make big profits from buying foreclosed residential property.

sion is to educate and train each investor on how to effectively profit from distressed and foreclosed real estate.

evelopment Partners in excess of $25,665,000 in wholesale real estate and current renovations to date; with future projects in estimated to reach $35,000,000.

n-house real estate been active in the acquisition, rehabilitation and liquidation of distressed properties since We are experts in all phases of real estate transactions, including locating profitable investments, fair market analysis, and property development and renovations.

25% return within 60 days with a minimum $5K investment. Call today for your free investment kit, or visit us on the web at www com.

Se habla Espanol.

The power to change your financial future.

I reate Our company has an excellent reputation for quality, reliability, and service. We are proud to be members of both the and th Since beginning in the business of developing have over 700 properties that have been purchased through wholesale and foreclosures throughout the metro area.

Invest now in the boomin rket, where you can buy investment properties and sell them within 60 days for a quick profit.

Chief Financial Officer

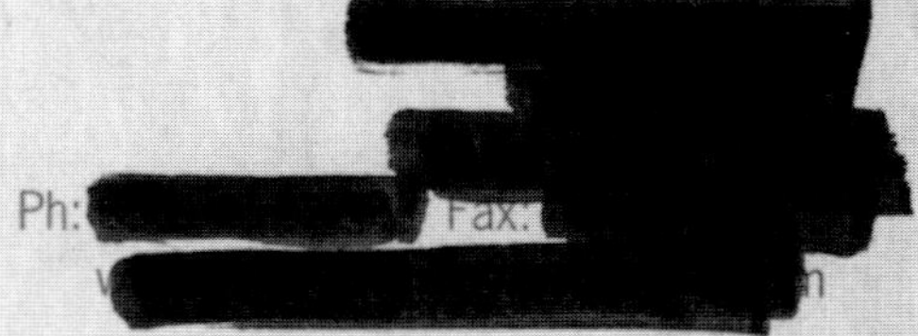

Ph: Fax:

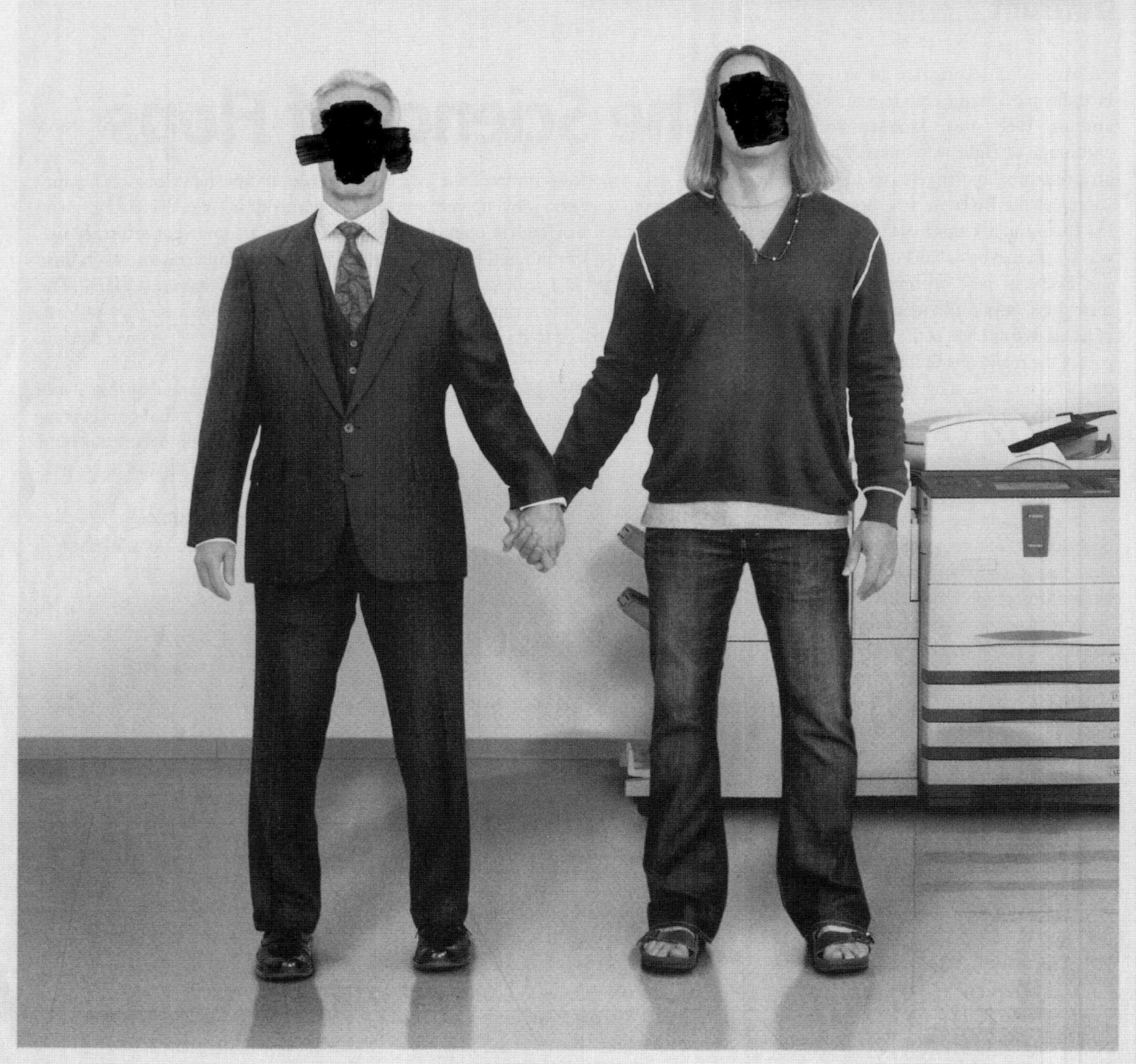

CFO & CIO

rings harmony into the boardroom. Number crunchers love the fact that they can save up to $350 per employee per year by eliminating unnecessary equipment. Tech geeks drool over the digital control they get when they can track everything with the click of a button. It's not world peace, but it's a start

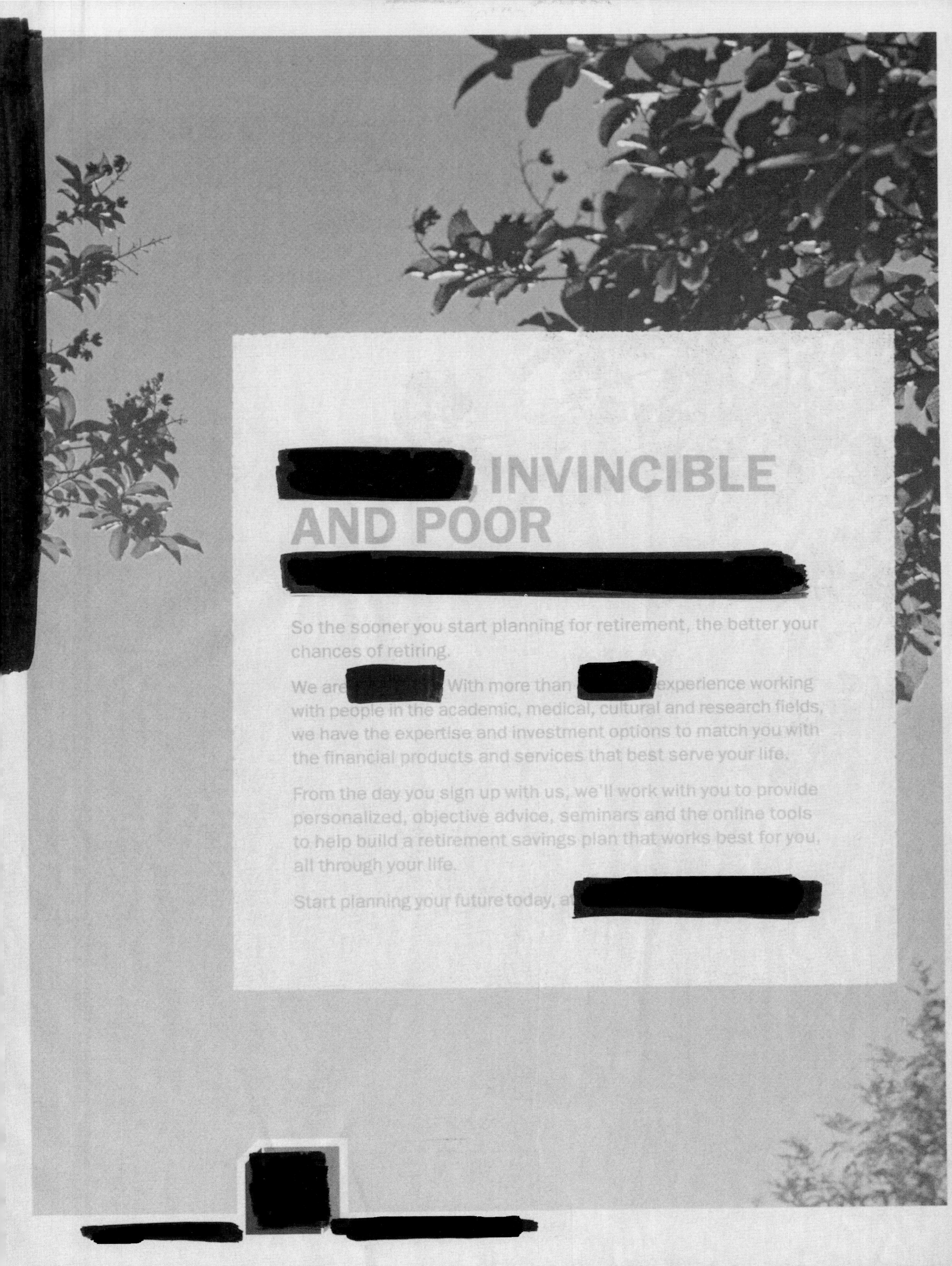
INVINCIBLE
AND POOR
So the sooner you start planning for retirement, the better your chances of retiring.
We are With more than experience working with people in the academic, medical, cultural and research fields, we have the expertise and investment options to match you with the financial products and services that best serve your life.
From the day you sign up with us, we'll work with you to provide personalized, objective advice, seminars and the online tools to help build a retirement savings plan that works best for you, all through your life.
Start planning your future today,

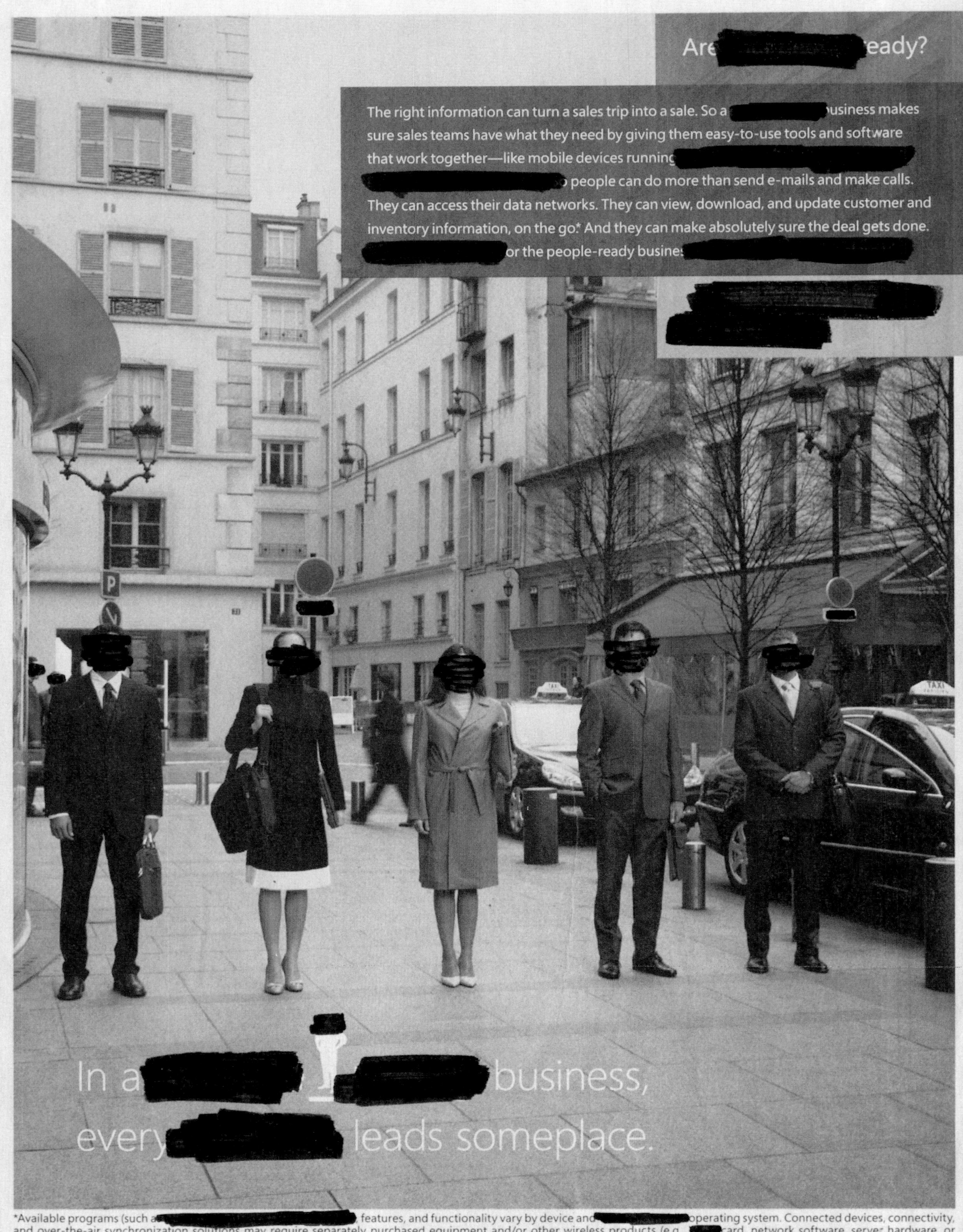

*Available programs (such a features, and functionality vary by device and operating system. Connected devices, connectivity, and over-the-air synchronization solutions may require separately purchased equipment and/or other wireless products (e.g., card, network software, server hardware, or redirector software). Service plans are required for and phone access. These products and services may need to be purchased separately. Features and performance may vary by service provider and are subject to network limitations. See device manufacturer, service provider, and/or corporate IT department for details.

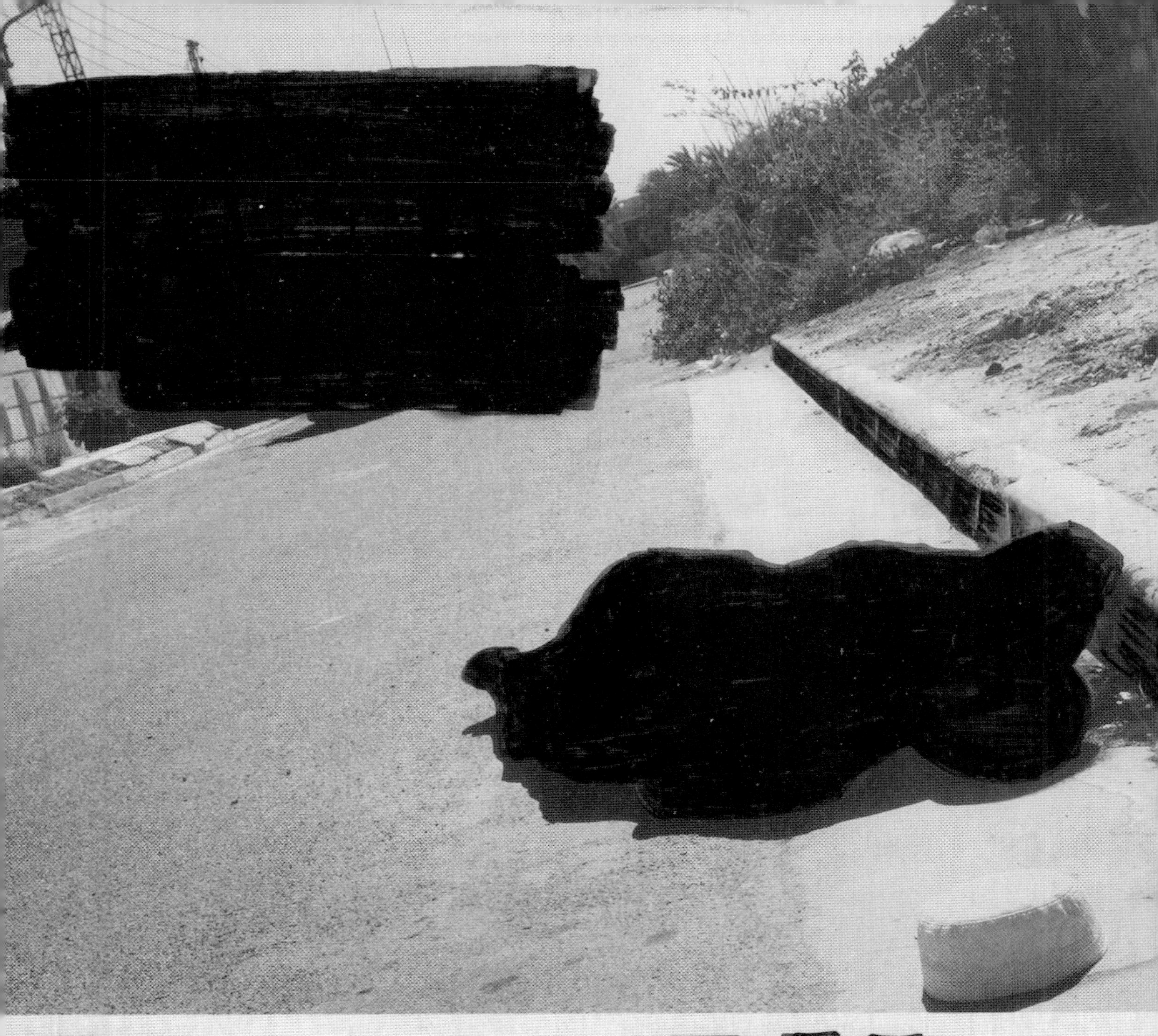

s focusing
attention o
at the hands
of But
have much more
to fear from their own
BY

TO UNDERSTAND JUST HOW , TH IN HAS BECOME, SPEND A
day at work wit , he travels to
the city of and
unknown —the scores o tha every day, bearing no
identifying characteristics save the method by which they we
On a typical trip to the last month
and a small band of volunteers unload the cargo they have brought
from the in an old flatbed truck. Sheathed in powder-
blue are the men, many of them bearing signs of
holes in the made by ,
burns. They are the signature of the shadow oups that have been
and most of them
a campaign that ha neighborhoods.

On any given inter by
("I can tell how close they were to th from t and
depth of th "), execution ("The are usually tied

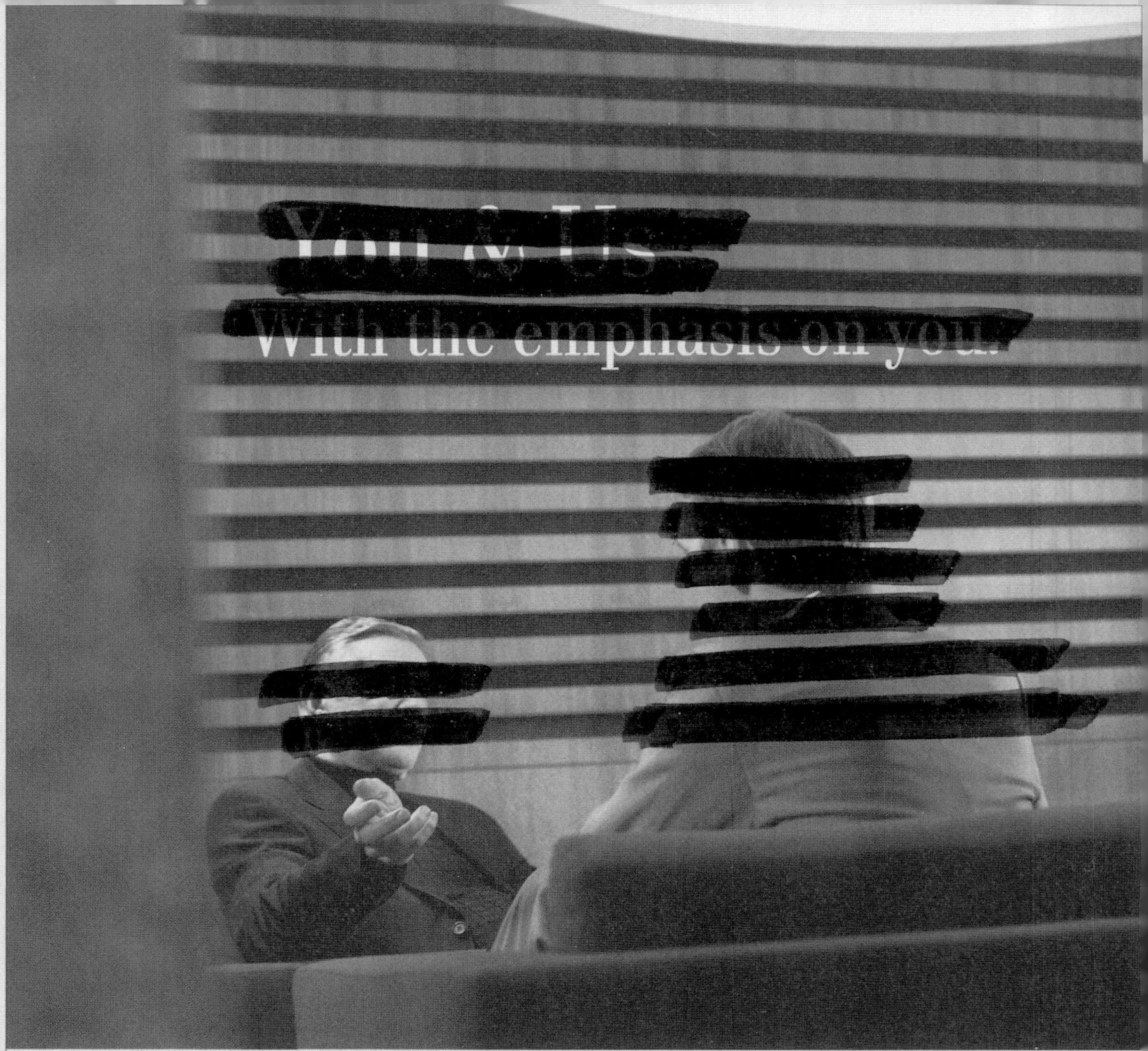

You & Us

With the emphasis on you.

A… we dedicate our resources to solving the financial issues that really matter. Yours. Our teams around the world research markets in depth. And our financial advisors devote the time it takes to understand your financial needs and goals in wealth management, asset management and investment banking. Then we connect the dots. It's a rigorous approach. But your financial issues demand nothing less.

Wealth | Global Asset | Investment

properties. Owners of a home, circa just got their annual taxes reduced from to when they signed a ten-year renewable preservation contract with the city.

On the other hand, let's say you want to get rid of the house. Call your home builders association and ask if any brokers specialize in teardowns. which sold the has offices Md. A competitor a Web site where sellers can list and buyers, usually builders, pay the 1%-to-3% commission.

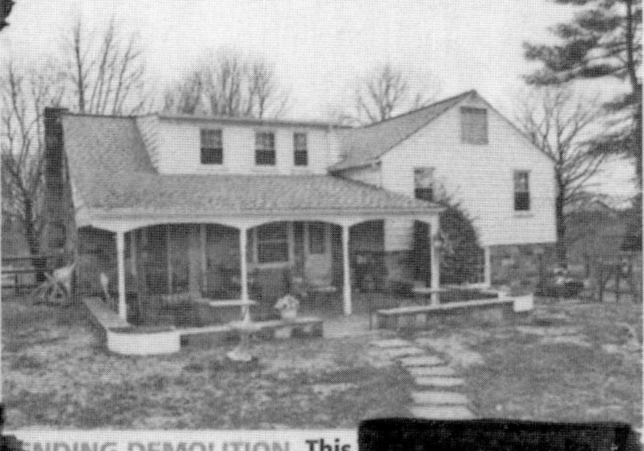

NDING DEMOLITION. This plit-level was the first on its

Take a field trip to your town's planning and zoning office and confirm for yourself what is your property's highest use—that is, what is the most that can be built on it. Don't count on a broker to get this information. When interviewed brokers to list his family's 2,200-square-foot ranch in they said they'd list it at $1.3 million, after fixed basement water problems and a fractured concrete walk as well as repainted a bedroom where the roof leaked.

Yet d done the buyer a favor by getting planning and zoning approval for an 8,800-square-foot replacement house. erties saw that permit as an asset and sold his property for $1,775,000 in February to a builder.

Finally, don't jump to the conclusion that your house is—or isn't—a teardown. If there have been no other teardowns in your neighborhood, gauging your home's potential may be tricky. You might find out that it's a teardown only after the fact.

That's what happened to giftware executive, who listed a split-level his parents built in ith and (with a 6% cut—ouch). The home needed a lot of work, which he wasn't eager to pay for. "Nobody thought of a developer," he says, but that's who bit just a few days after ted it in The builder paid $650,000 cash, close to the asking price—no inspection, no repairs. He bought the house next door and is putting up two new $1.7 million houses.

was happy to be rid of the property and get the deal done fast. His advice to other owners of tired houses: Find a Realtor to market the house as a teardown for a reduced commission. If that fails, kick back and relax when a builder bites.

the crowd of [illegible] refugees. "An entire generation of people."

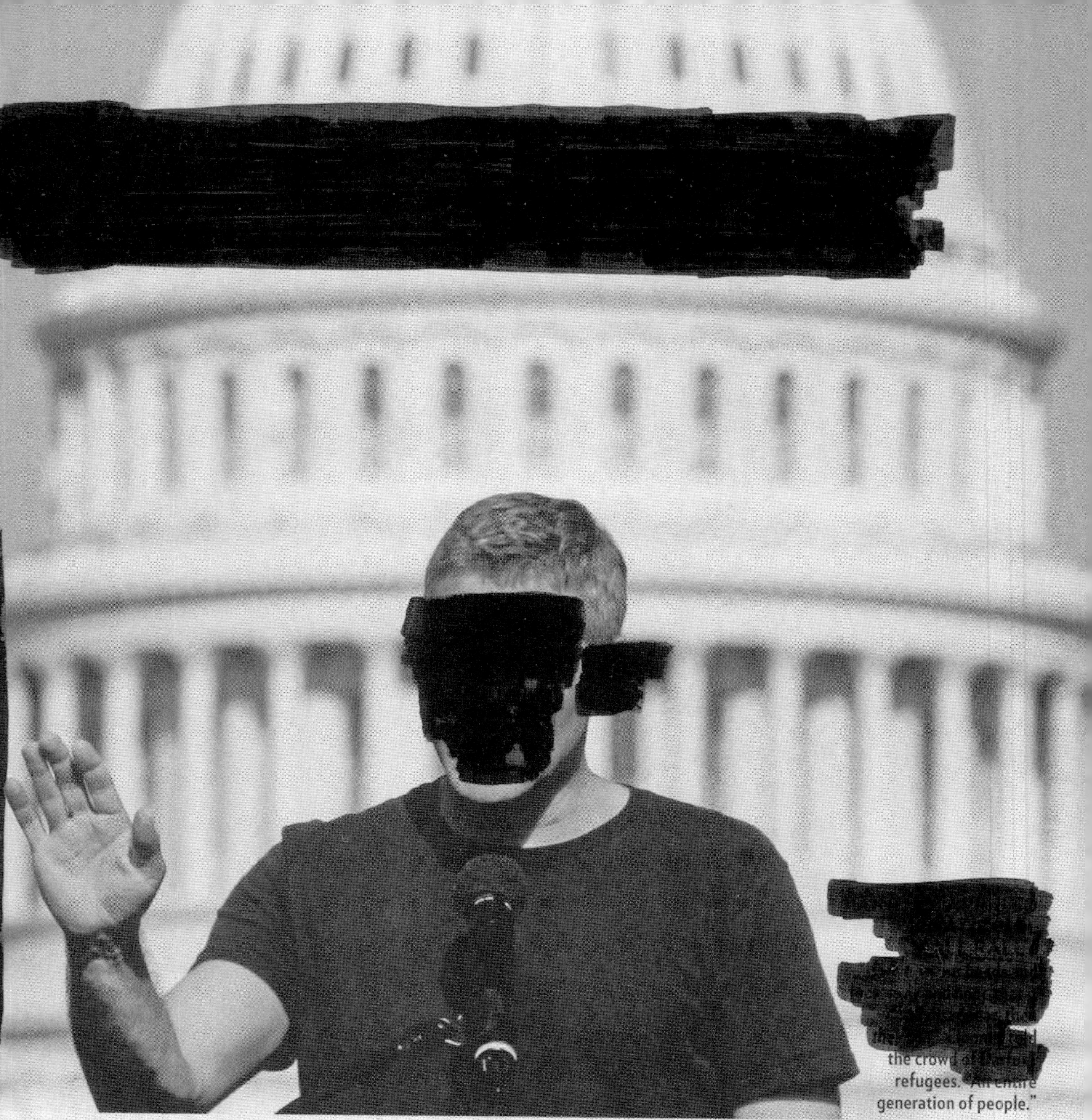

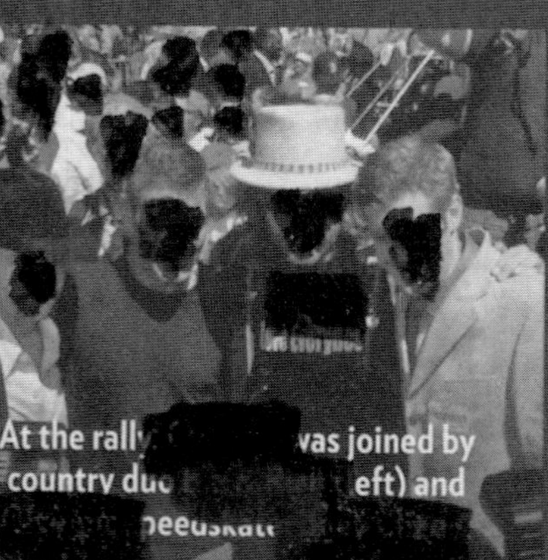

At the rally [illegible] was joined by [illegible] country duo [illegible] (left) and [illegible] speedskater [illegible]

WHAT YOU [illegible]

For three years unrest between [illegible] militias and [illegible] ethnic groups has left around [illegible] and [illegible] homeless in [illegible] a remote region in [illegible] [illegible] Rwanda," said [illegible] dad. "This one, we can stop." How? Activists urge [illegible]s to visit [illegible], where individuals can donate money for refugees and petition the [illegible] to increase funds to international peacekeepers.

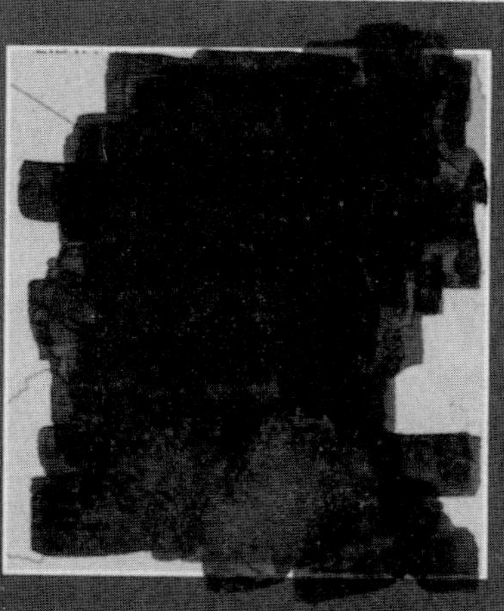

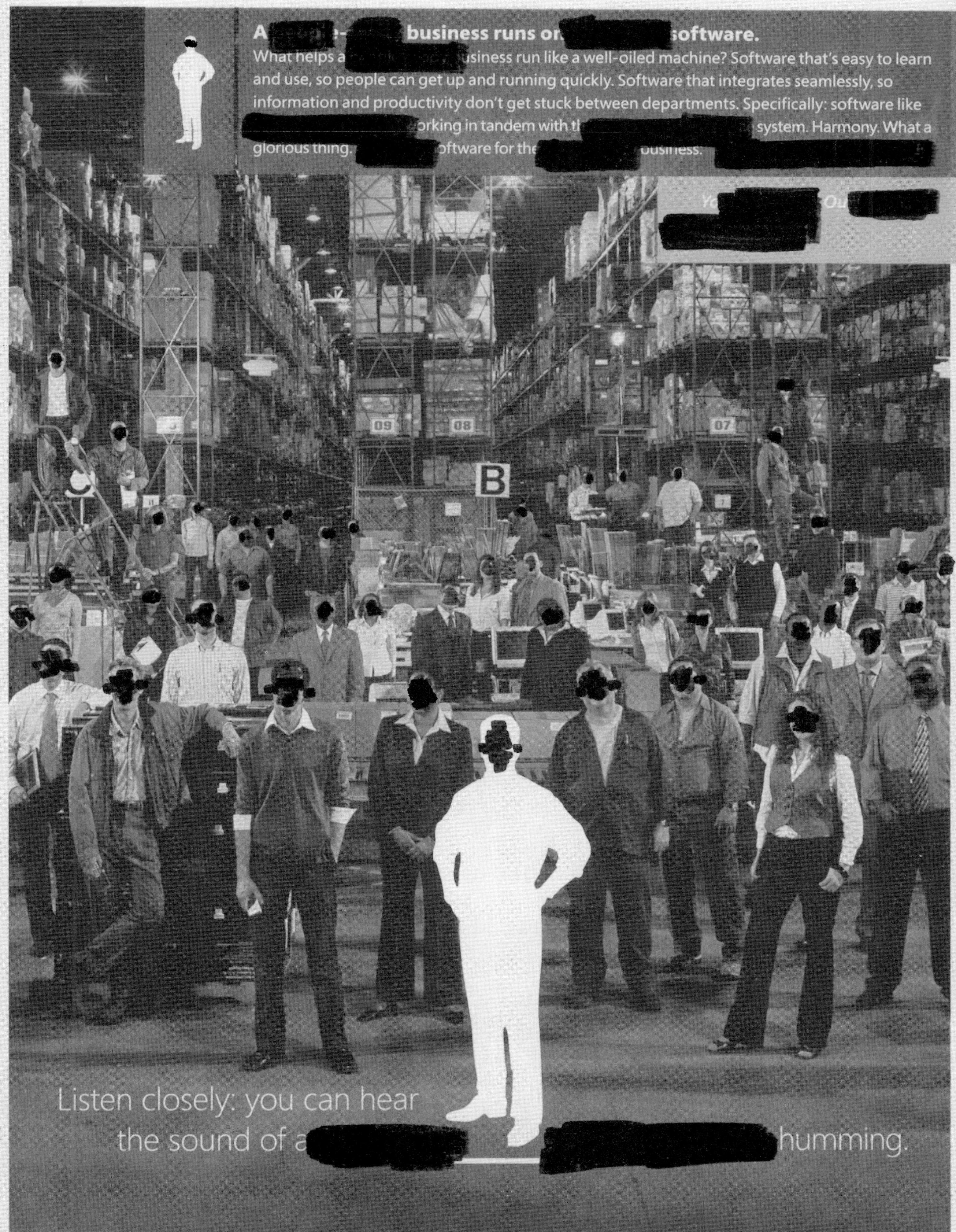

A business runs on software.
What helps a business run like a well-oiled machine? Software that's easy to learn and use, so people can get up and running quickly. Software that integrates seamlessly, so information and productivity don't get stuck between departments. Specifically: software like
orking in tandem with th system. Harmony. What a glorious thing. oftware for the business.
09
08
07
B
Listen closely: you can hear
the sound of a humming.

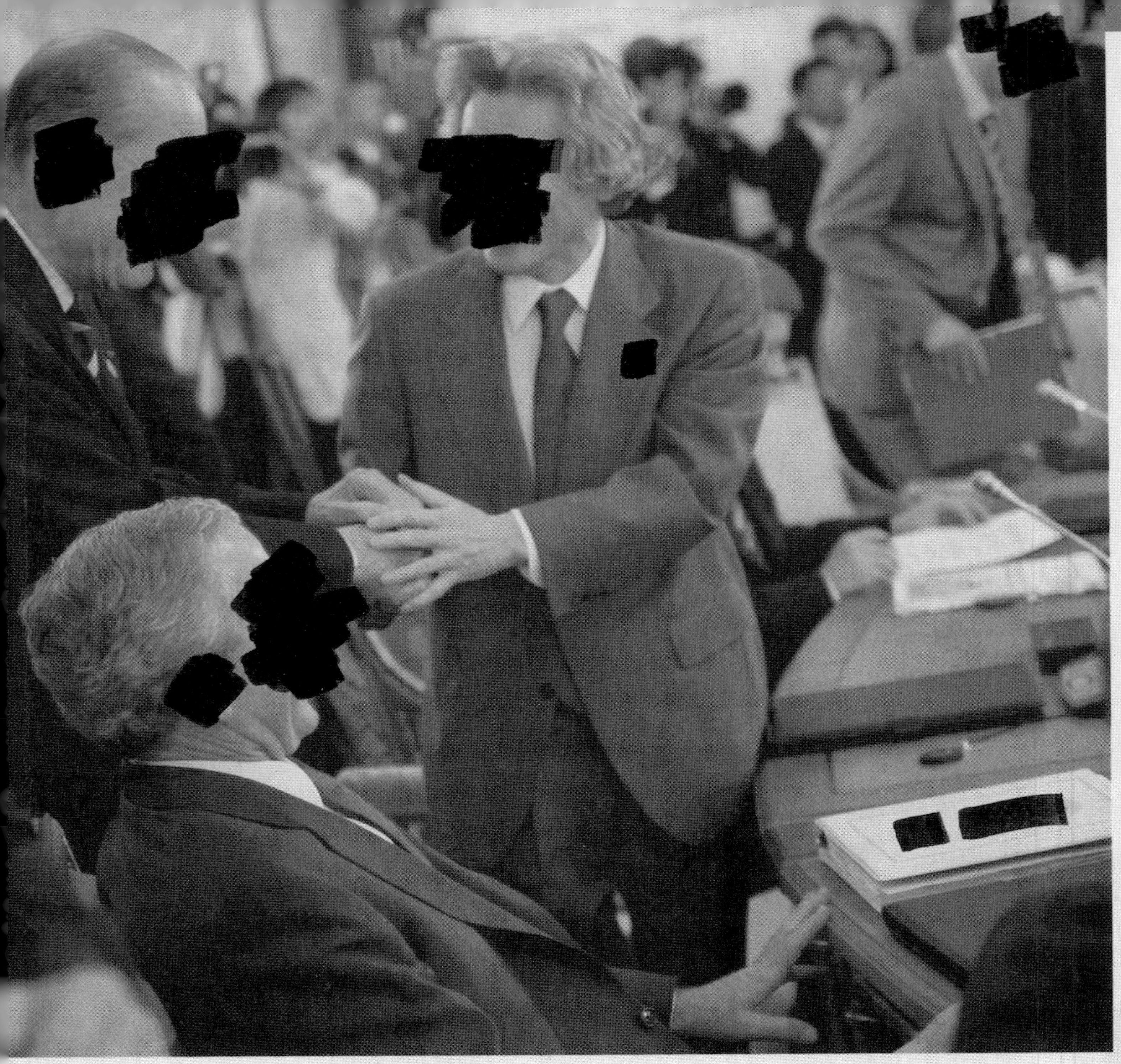

senior aides, spending hours behind the security curtain that surrounds in the air and on the ground. Between meetings with world leaders, agreed to four freewheeling interviews and hundreds of candid photographs. He showed his ease with diplomacy on his terms—in short one-on-one meetings that he could control. But he also showed his impatience with the formal statecraft of summits and group sessions, where his voice was just one among many. In the interviews, he was unusually relaxed, revealing a president by turns playful and pensive, stubborn and accommodating, as he grappled with the biggest foreign crisis of his second term.

A CALL FROM ON HIGH

IN THE TWO DAYS SINCE HE LEFT THE has wooed the new and enjoyed feasting on wild boar. His aides, meanwhile, were busy with the crisis: gathering intel, shuttling across the region and strategizing about the way ahead. On the ground, airport runways and flattened headquarters in the city in re- has fired rockets a city and struck an warship on the coast.

Now it's time for to intervene.

Again aboard , en route from to the summit in sits in his long wood-paneled conference room and His two advisers have been gaming out possible twists and turns in the crisis, calling intelligence and military officials to get a jump on the enemy's next move. One question arises early on. Should call After all, he is a close ally and friend. But in the delicate diplomacy of the direct talks could easily backfire. does call the press will want to know what they discussed. doesn't want to look raised on anger and fear, are potentially rebels without clear causes. "What will their jihads become?" he asks. "Are they going to grow up to kill each other, or will they turn their weapons against the West?" If somehow peace can be won, they may give up their guns, sa[illegible] most of those in the war generations of [illegible] and the [illegible] have done in recent memory.

But what's clear is that we're far closer to the beginning of this cycle of violence than to its en[illegible] is not known to have specifically appealed to [illegible] kids, and most intelligence warnings about the conflict there have focused on the adult jihadists who are gaining on-the-ground experience in the fight. But radical groups have always found their most ready recruits in societies undergoing profound and violent change. The closest analogy may be to th[illegible] in[illegible]. They filled their ranks with the orphans of war—very often refugee kids—and offered them a different kind of family structure cemented by the bonds [illegible] is full of such kids. A[illegible] 14-year-old [illegible] about soccer or computer games and the gangly boy's finely featured face lights up—brief moments of respite from the burden he so clearly bears. On a warm [illegible] evening [illegible] and his father [illegible] were closing up their clothing shop in the sout[illegible] district [illegible]. Suddenly an unknown man stepped out of a car parked nearby and, without warning, fired a handgun into [illegible] head and body—12 shots, until the magazine was empty. "I still remember the sound of the bullets," says [illegible] "It's like a dream to me." He fled, [illegible] deep into the city. His family could not find him for hours.

Even now, a year and a half later, [illegible] sometimes succumbs to fits of anxiety that his family members quell by holding him down and feeding him sedatives they buy at the local pharmacy. Sadly, his story is not exceptional. [illegible] by [illegible] psychiatrists, sponsored in part by the [illegible] found that 30 percent of the 1,090 children surveyed at schools in [illegible] are suffering from post-traumatic stress disorder. In [illegible] 47 percent of those surveyed reported exposure to a major traumatic event," and 14 percent suffered from symptoms of PTSD. These can include anxiety, depression and nightmares—all of which are particularly damaging to young minds. "Some children wake up in the middle of the night and can't go back to sleep, [worried about] how they're going to school in the morning," says [illegible] who works with an [illegible] aid group called [illegible] "Is there going to be someone in the street waiting to kill or kidnap them?" In [illegible] study published by the [illegible] of [illegible] percent of the kids surveyed showed signs of learning impediments.

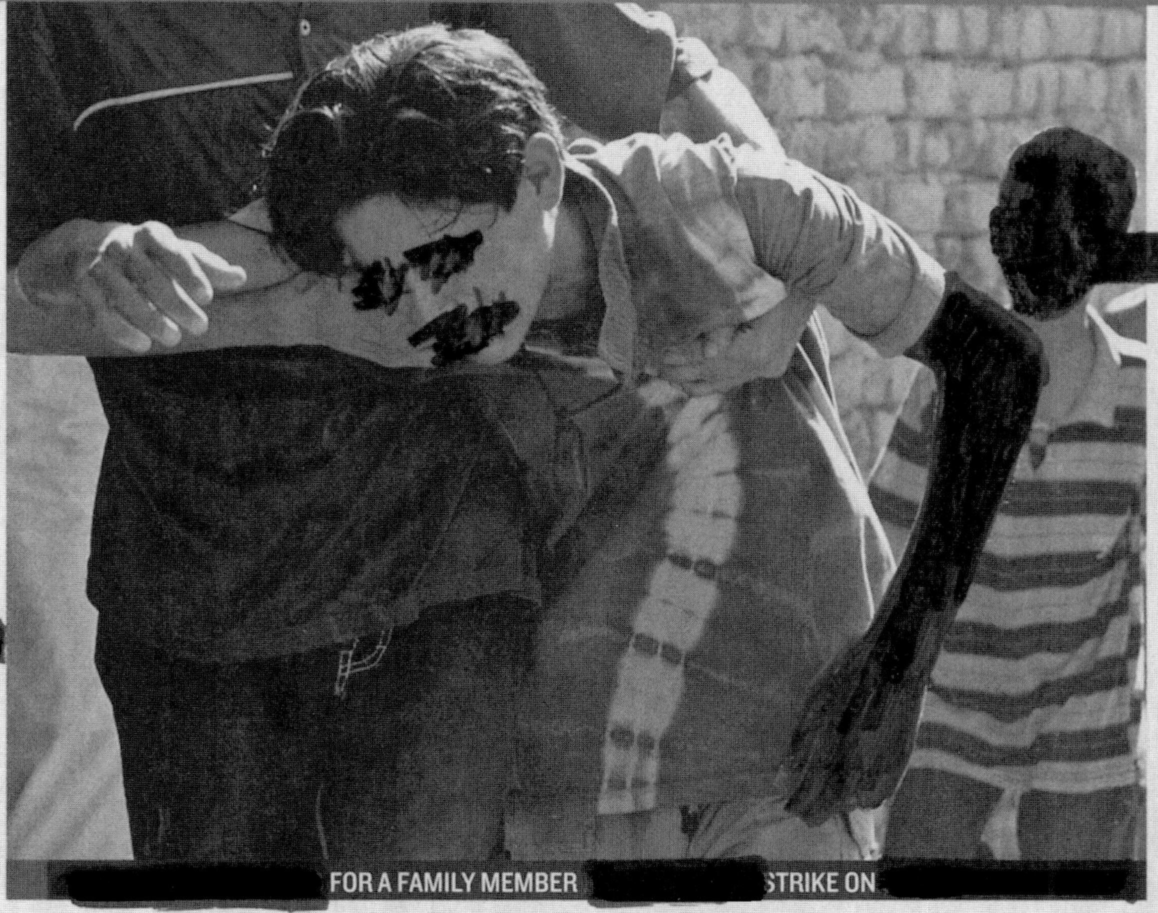

[illegible] FOR A FAMILY MEMBER [illegible] STRIKE ON [illegible]

In one survey of [illegible] in the [illegible] capital, some [illegible] of respondents said they'd witnessed a [illegible]

[illegible] is typical in another sense: he has joined the growing hordes [illegible] displaced within the country, who now number as many as [illegible] according to the [illegible] family are [illegible] and before his father's killing they had received anonymous threats warning them to leave their home in predominantly [illegible]. Now they find themselves living in [illegible] district where they know no one. [illegible] neighborhoods used to be close-knit places where neighbors shared information and helped out each other regardless of sect or ethnicity. Parents watched after each other's kids; the children had a ready support network. Today, often scarred like [illegible] refugees are surrounded by strangers thrown together by sect and defended by militias.

Once wrecked, these families have little capacity to rebound. While no reliable figures of kids orphaned or left fatherless by the war exist, the overwhelming majority of [illegible] civilians killed in the sectarian slaughter have been men between the ages of 18 and 40. The [illegible] says it's been seeing a stark increase in the number of households run by women—a problem in traditional [illegible] society, where women rarely work outside the home. In [illegible] 17-year-old [illegible] had to become the primary breadwinner for his family after his father went into hiding, wanted by the [illegible]. He still attends high school in the mornings, but then drives a taxi to earn money. "I'm exhausted," the tall, athletic teen says, sighing. "At my age it's hard to bear all these miseries and concerns." A 20-year-old cousin now supports [illegible] extended family of 11 people, once com

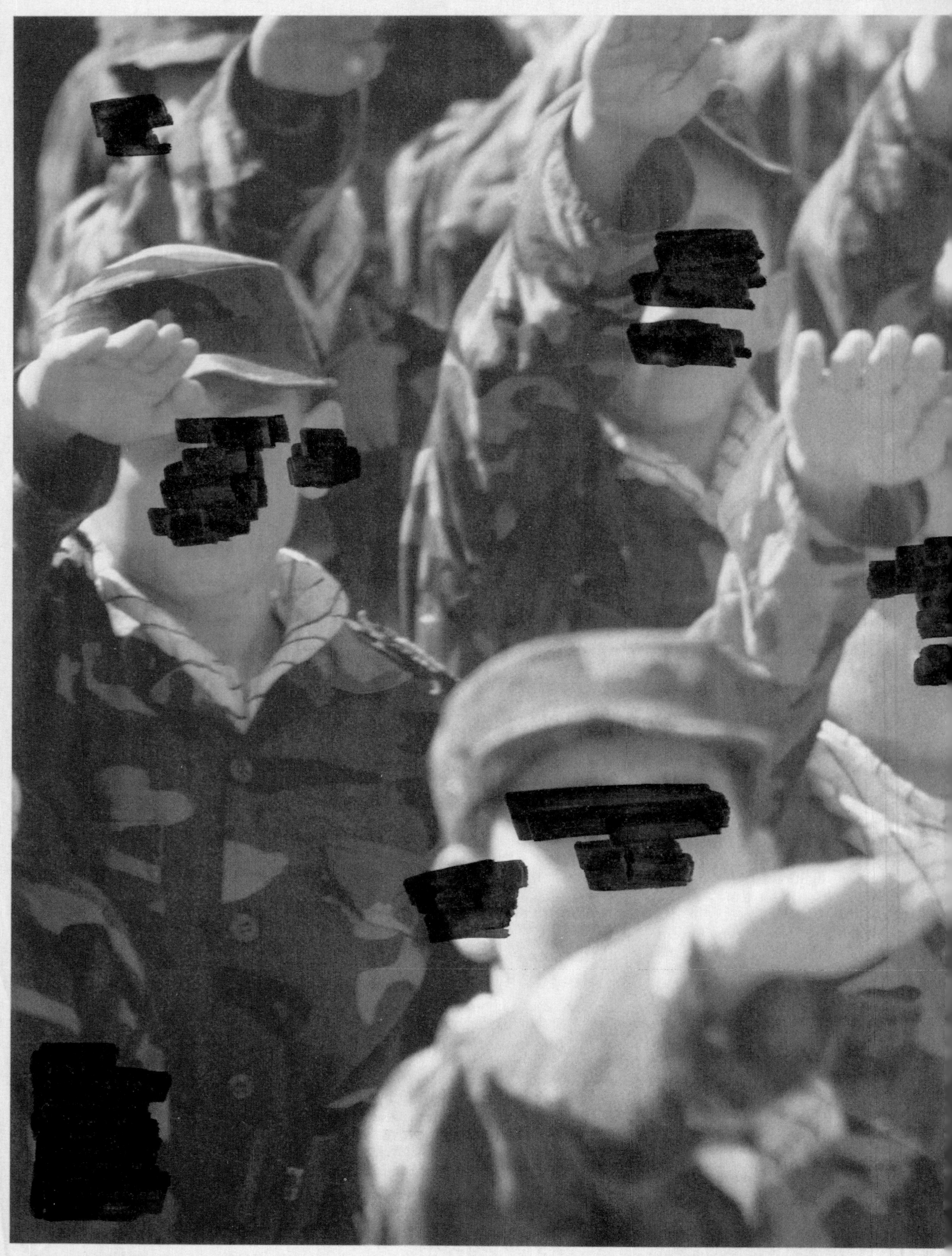

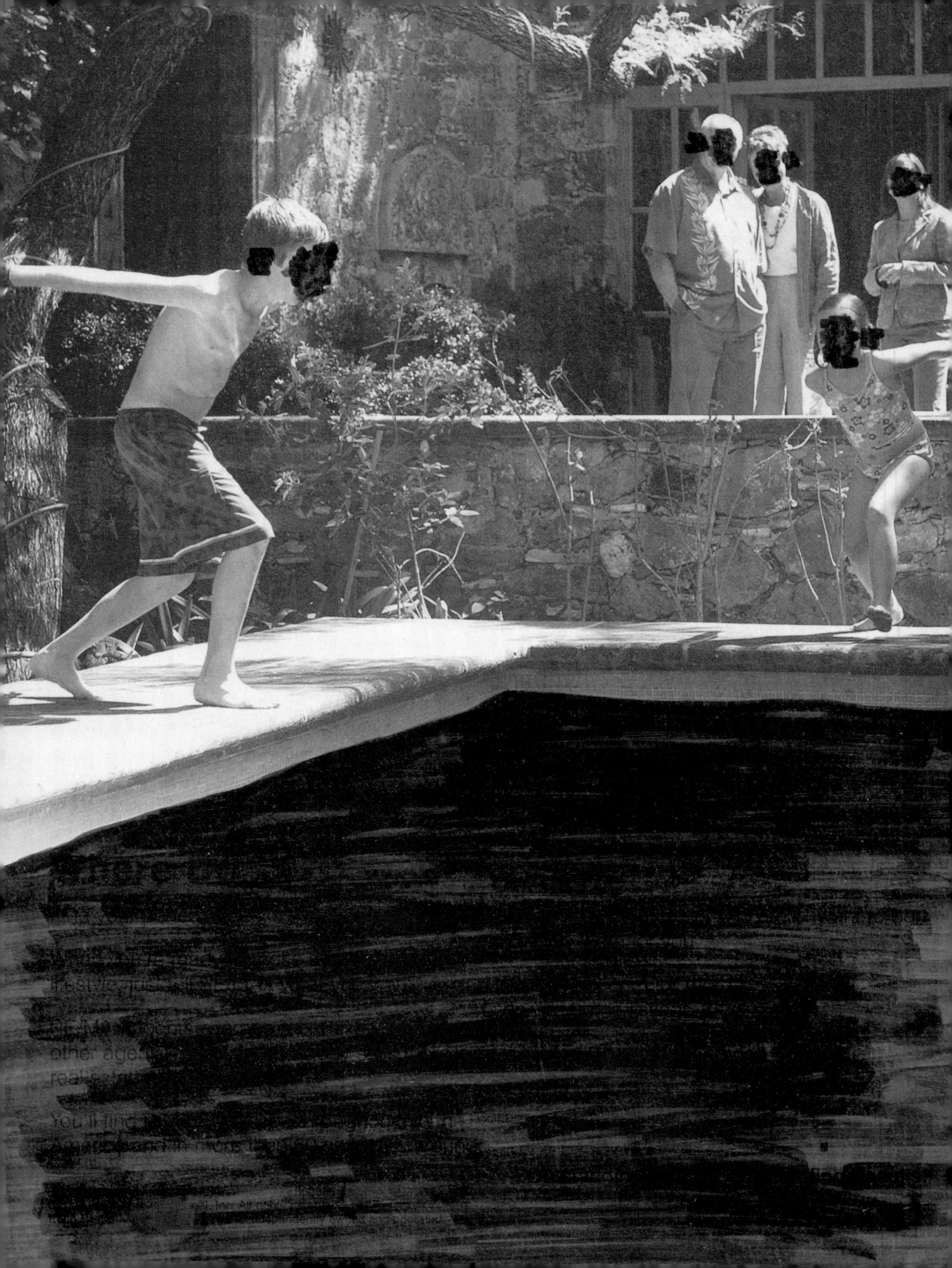

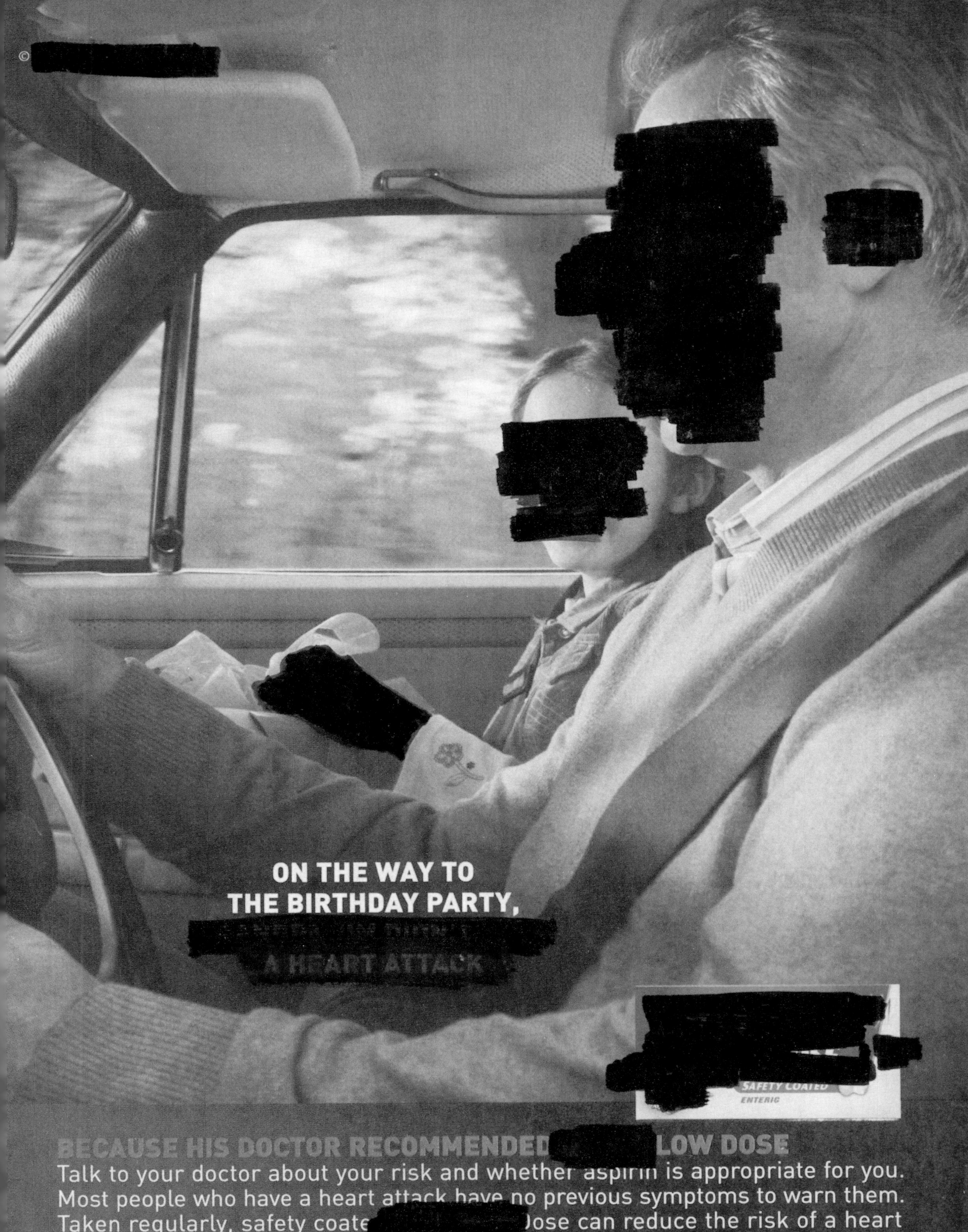
ON THE WAY TO
THE BIRTHDAY PARTY,
SAFETY COATED
ENTERIC
BECAUSE HIS DOCTOR RECOMMENDED
LOW DOSE
Talk to your doctor about your risk and whether aspirin is appropriate for you.
Most people who have a heart attack have no previous symptoms to warn them.
Taken regularly, safety coate
Dose can reduce the risk of a heart
attack by 32%. Aspirin is not appropriate for everyone so be sure to talk to your doctor before you begin an aspirin regimen.

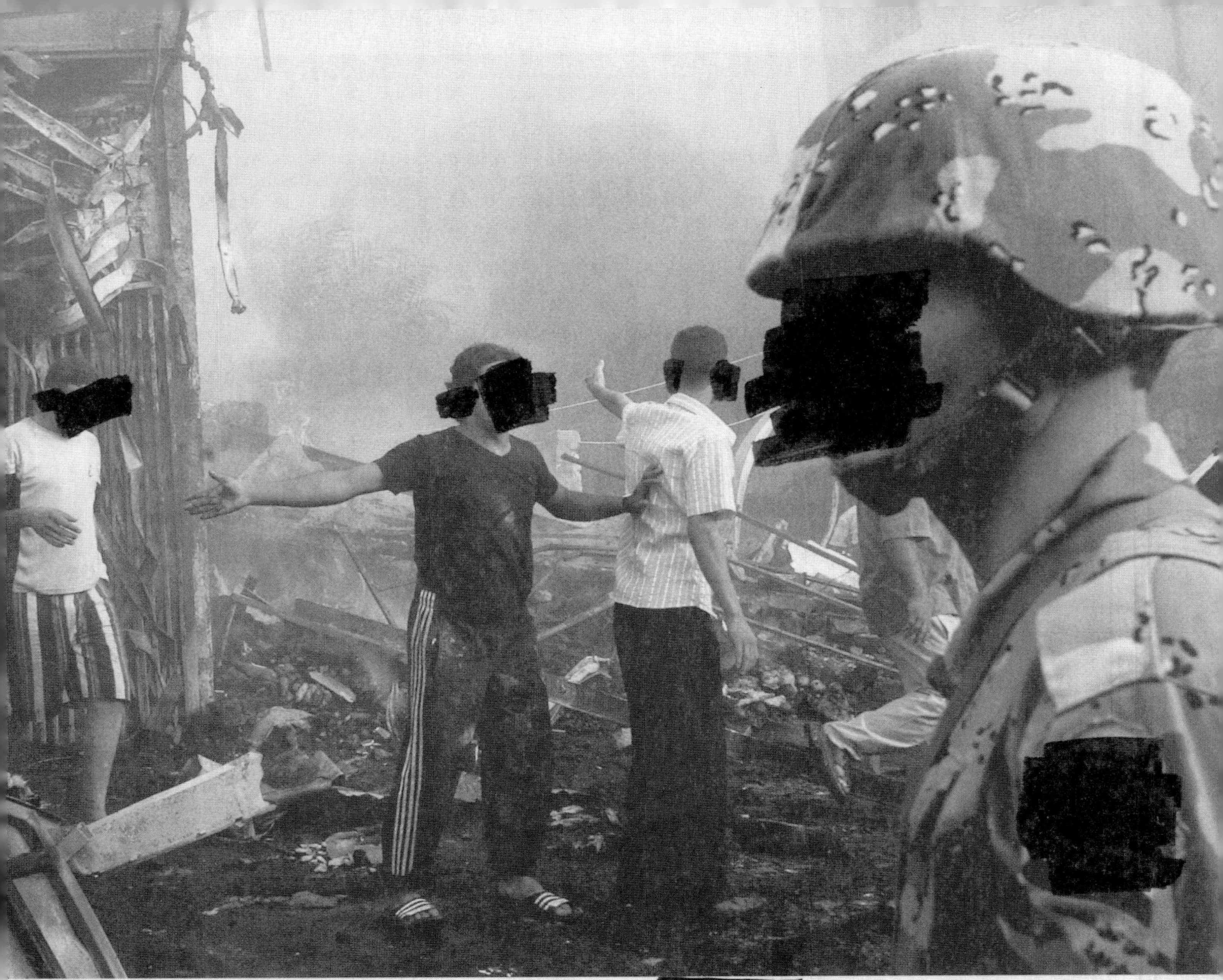

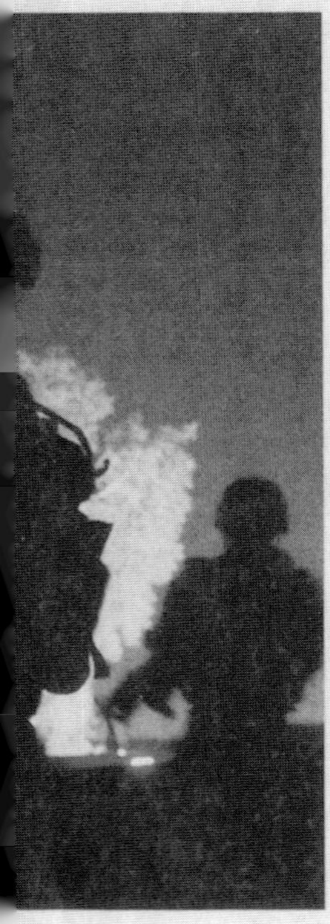

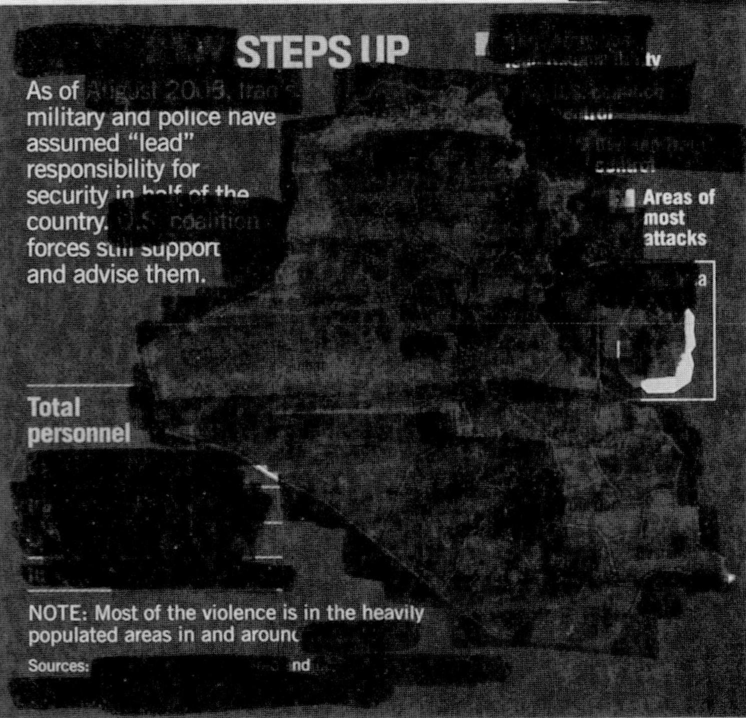

achieving the fundamental requirements for peace, many commanders say. Among their principal complaints: A political reconciliation pact has not been achieved. Too little has been spent on reconstruction and services to win over ordinary and too few of the troops are being used to mentor security forces.

The lack of security is only the most obvious symptom of the lack of progress. Even armed soldiers cannot move around any more freely than they could a year or two ago. They travel from dad's airport to downtown on high-speed choppers or on a hulking armored bus called the . Riders don helmets and bulletproof vests for the midnight rides. Drivers wearing night-vision goggles pilot the with headlights off, in a convoy guarded by bristling with heavy-caliber guns and escorted by attack aircraft.

Resupply convoys still roll mostly in the dead of night, snaking out of military

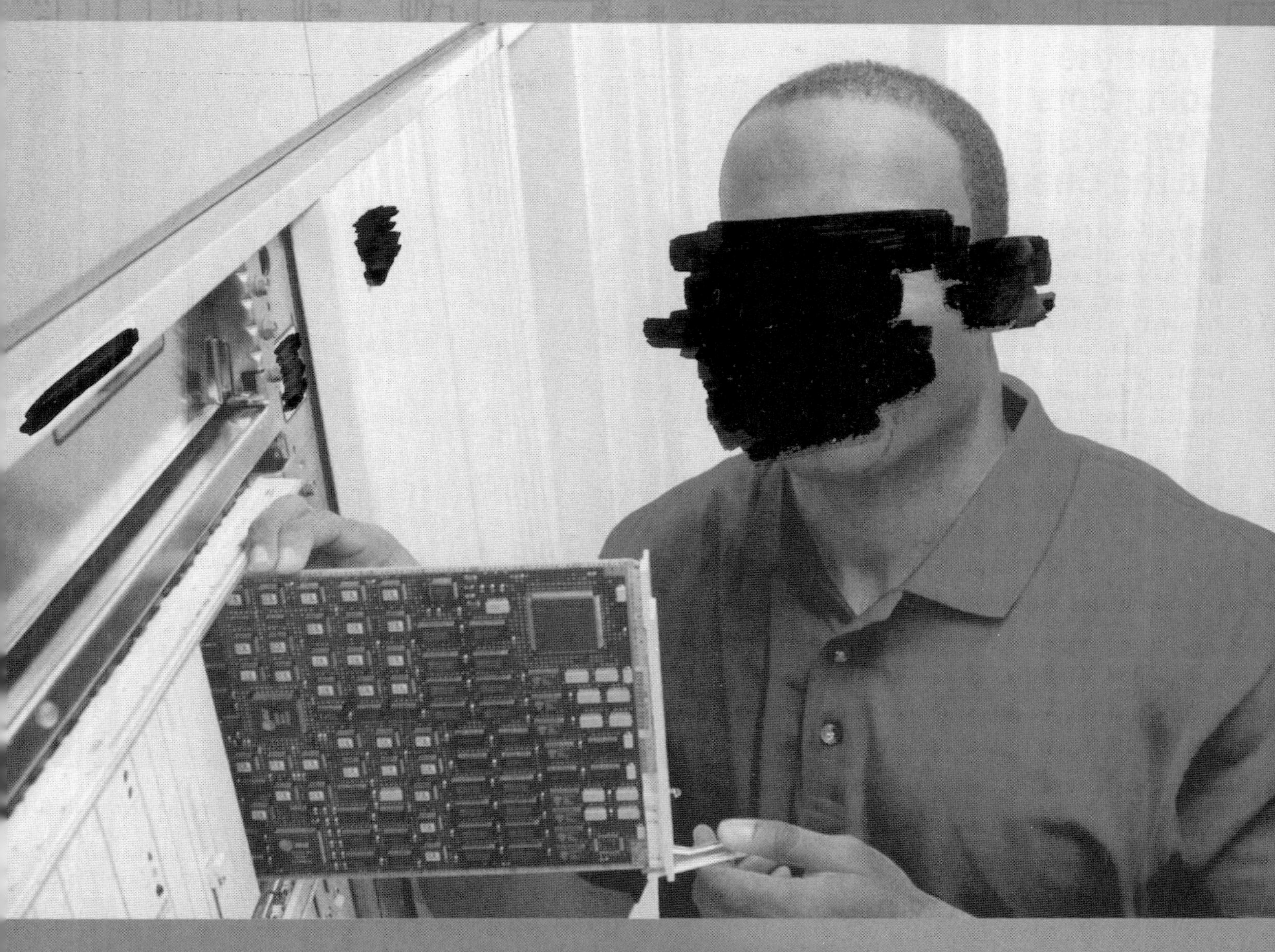

why do i like working here?

great feeling, the best experience s making the latest technology real pleasure

improve myself, performance incentives flexibility

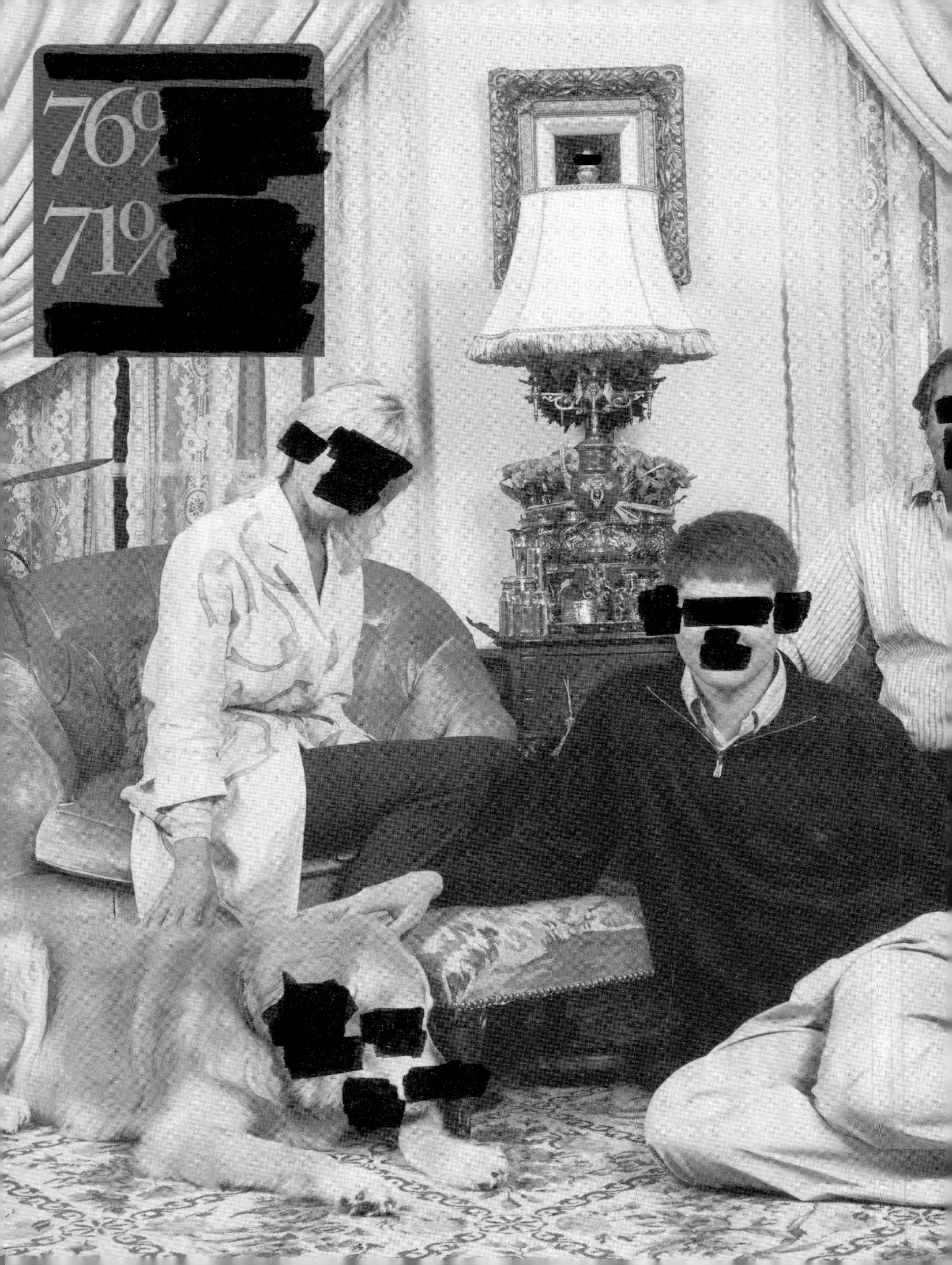
76
71%

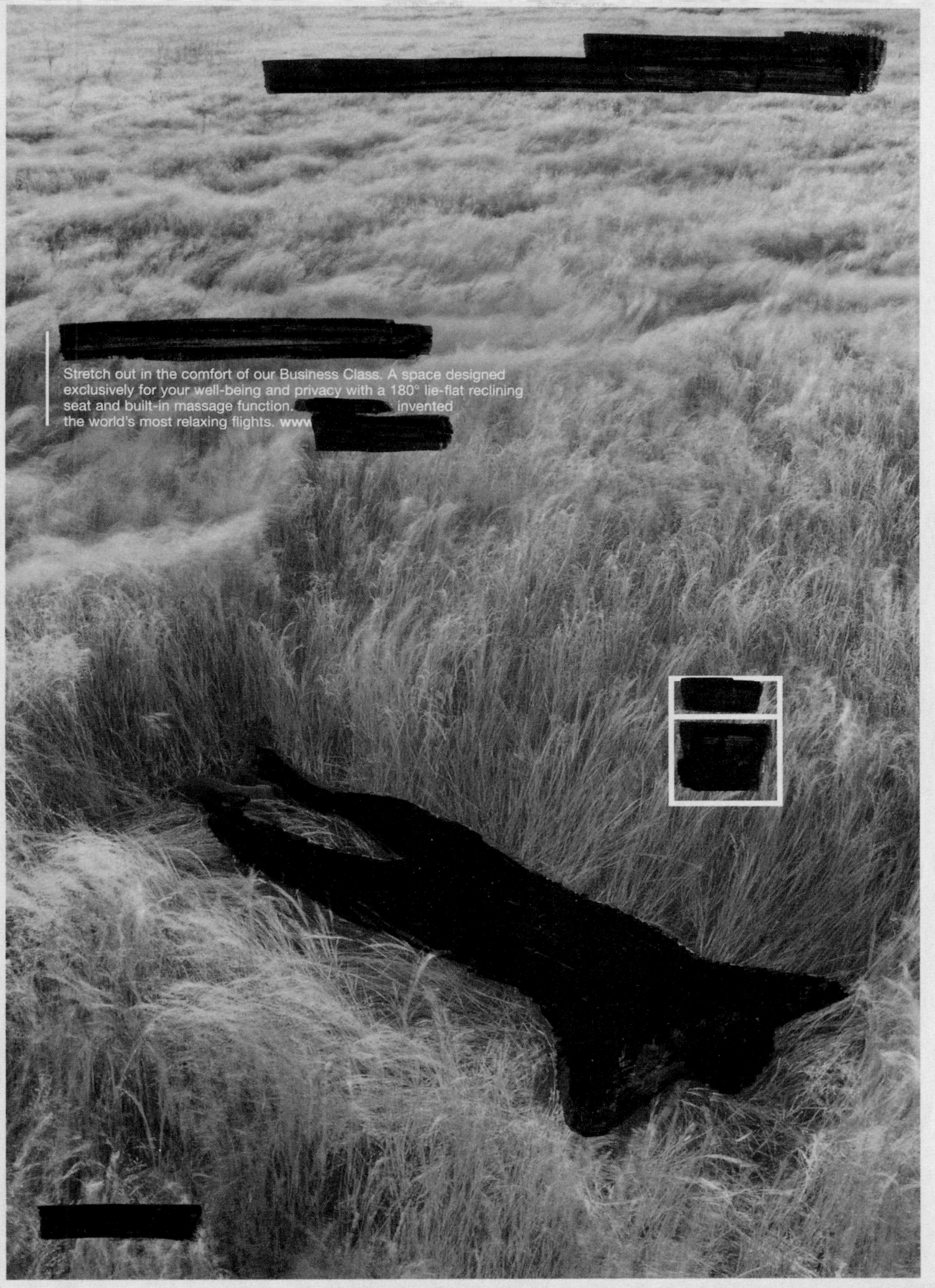
Stretch out in the comfort of our Business Class. A space designed
exclusively for your well-being and privacy with a 180° lie-flat reclining
seat and built-in massage function. invented
the world's most relaxing flights. www

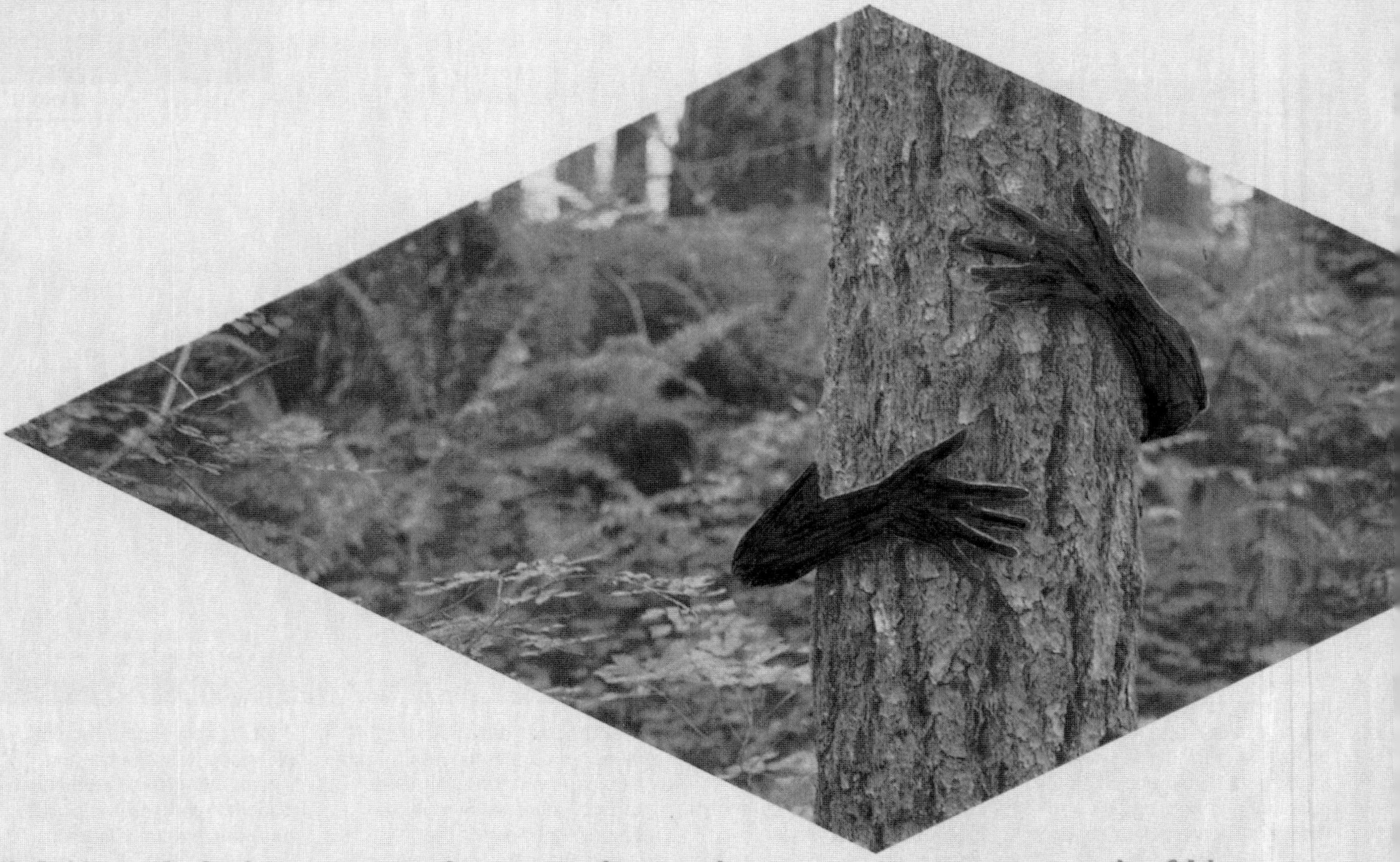

Who'd have thought that a natural fiber could help fight

Well actually, we did.

You gotta love nature. Example: Cellulose fiber, the most abundant, renewable carbohydrate found in nature, can be used to help prevent M dietary fiber is made from natural cellulose. In tests scientists and th found that adding a few grams of to a high-fat diet slowed fat absorption, potentially reducing the development of – a precursor to The availability of in the foods we buy will make it easy to get the fiber we need. Cutting our fat and sugar intake wouldn't hurt either. See how s using the right chemistry to help protect our health at

Health

Lifestyle

Communication

Transportation

Building

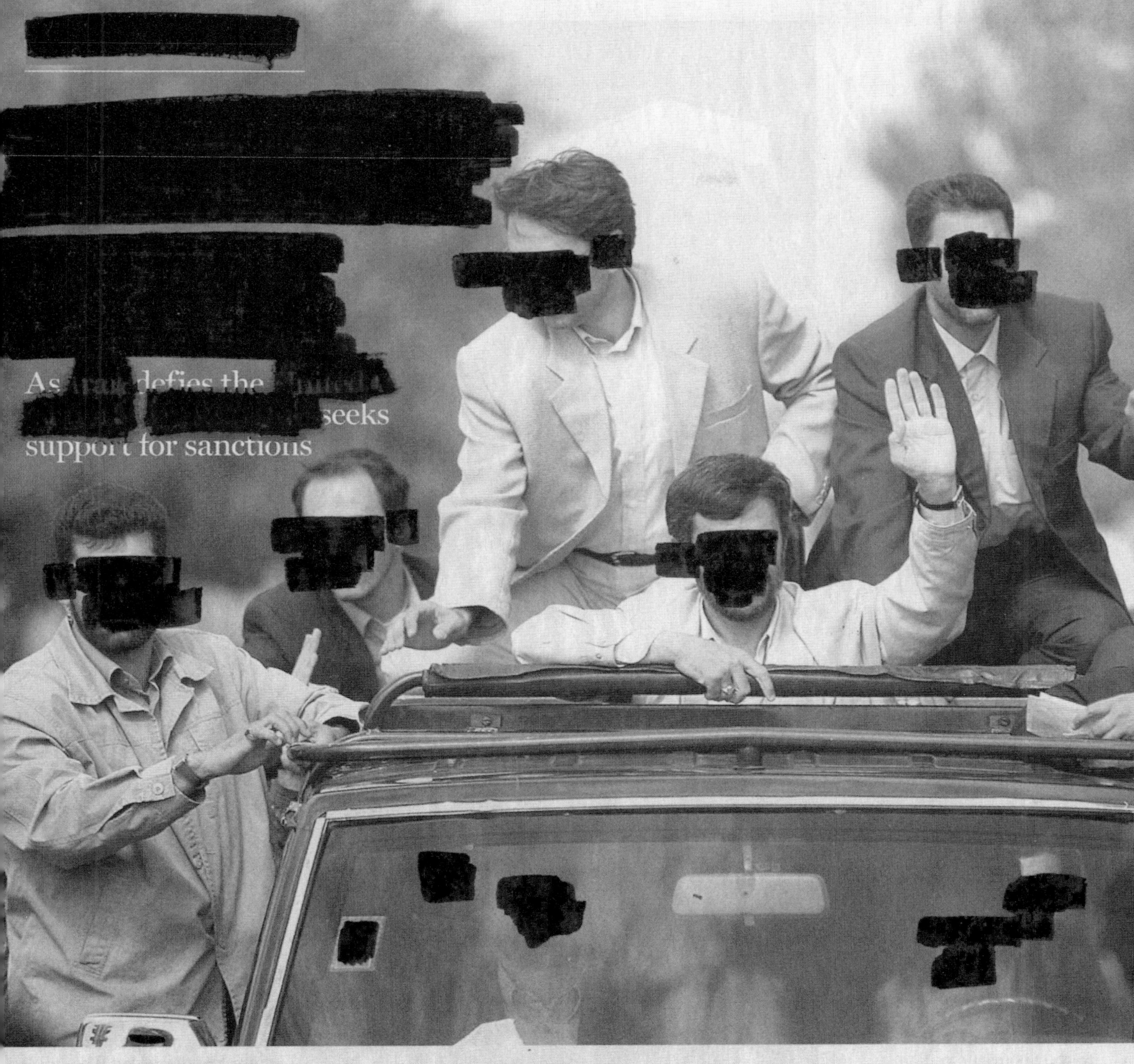

As defies the seeks support for sanctions

By

They didn't say "Yes," but they didn't exactly say "No" either. The long-awaited response last week by aders to an incentive-laced package intended to lure th way from making nuclear fuel left the countries offering it frustrated once again—and searching for a way to move forward together in the face of eft maneuvering.

The complicated reply had diplomats from the nd uzzling over their translated texts, sifting through what one called an occasionally contradictory set of comments and queries. pitched its response as comprehensive, as a gateway to immediate, "serious" talks. But it was clear that had chosen to reject the core demand of th owers, rendered legally binding by a esolution: to halt o by a deadline of wants to start negotiating on says a official.

delay. That approach is already sparking moves by the administration and some governments to win approval for sanctions. "We're " of getting sanctions, says the Those could include banning the sale to gear and dual-use technology, a visa ban on travel by officials, and a freeze on some financial accounts.

But gaining . approval will likely prove trying, even though officials have said that nd already agree in principle to support some sanctions if carries on past the end of The and acceptance followed concessions by , including a willingness to negotiate directly over the andoff and to support two communities. Caught in the middle, the military is unable to halt the bloodshed. is right: news these days is all bad.

As a result, have little time for other people's tragedies. The news from has dominated channels like recent weeks, but it hasn't resonated much with Politicians, especially leaders with ties to, have issued predictable broadsides against some, like the radical cleric have blamed the too. He orchestrated a large demonstration in his stronghold last week—a protest against the bombing in but also a piece of political theater designed to showcase the strength of his support (and a response to a muscle-flexing rally organized earlier by a rival). For the most part, ordinary although sympathetic to their coreligionists in have shown little interest in a conflict that seems both far away and from another era—a leftover war from the Not only are the protagonists familiar, but so too are their tactics and weapons rtillery rockets.

Those looking for parallels in will find few. The war in about century issues, like terrorism and extremist The very survival of a nation hangs in the balance. It is a murky battlefield, where combatants are hard to identify and alliances shift constantly, so nothing and nobody are predictable. Even the weapons are postmodern: improvised explosive devices, car bombs, suicide bombers. And the is far deadlier; on almost any given day, casualty figures in alone dwarf those in an combined. At the house uses as its base in our staff of snort disdainfully as news broadcasters announce the daily death toll in the "They count their dead in dozens. We count ours in hundreds," says our bureau manager. Only when bombs killed eople in the village of did it register on s radar. Watching the images of the carnage, he declares, "Now they know ho e."

EVERY SO OFTEN, SOMETHING HAPPENS THAT CAUSES the government and the to announce that a turning point has arrived for the beleaguered country. In the month that I was away from there were two such events: the killing of terrorist and the appointment, after weeks of political haggling, of new ministers of The ministers, a an respectively, had been touted as independent and nonsectarian—new brooms to brush away the rampant corruption in the two crucial security ministries. Interior, in particular, would be cleansed of the militias that had infiltrated all levels of the police and other security forces and turned them into instruments of vengeance against their former ppressors.

The ministers were the last bricks on the façade that is the all-party national-unity government of Earlier in the year I had watched from close quarters as ma worked tirelessly to make that government possible, pleading, cajoling until all the political factions— nd secular—agreed to get in the big tent together. Relieved, the announced that the participation of all groups, especially the recalcitrant would allow government to succeed where the military had failed, in bringing to heel both the insurgency and the rising might of the militias. Never mind that the was himself a artisan until his nomination—whereupon he sought to reinvent himself as a nonsectarian leader—and that his party had stronger ties to than to An ornery figure, al- is a backroom politician plainly ill at ease in public; few had even heard of him, and few are convinced that his rancorous all-party government can last the year, much less its full four-year term.

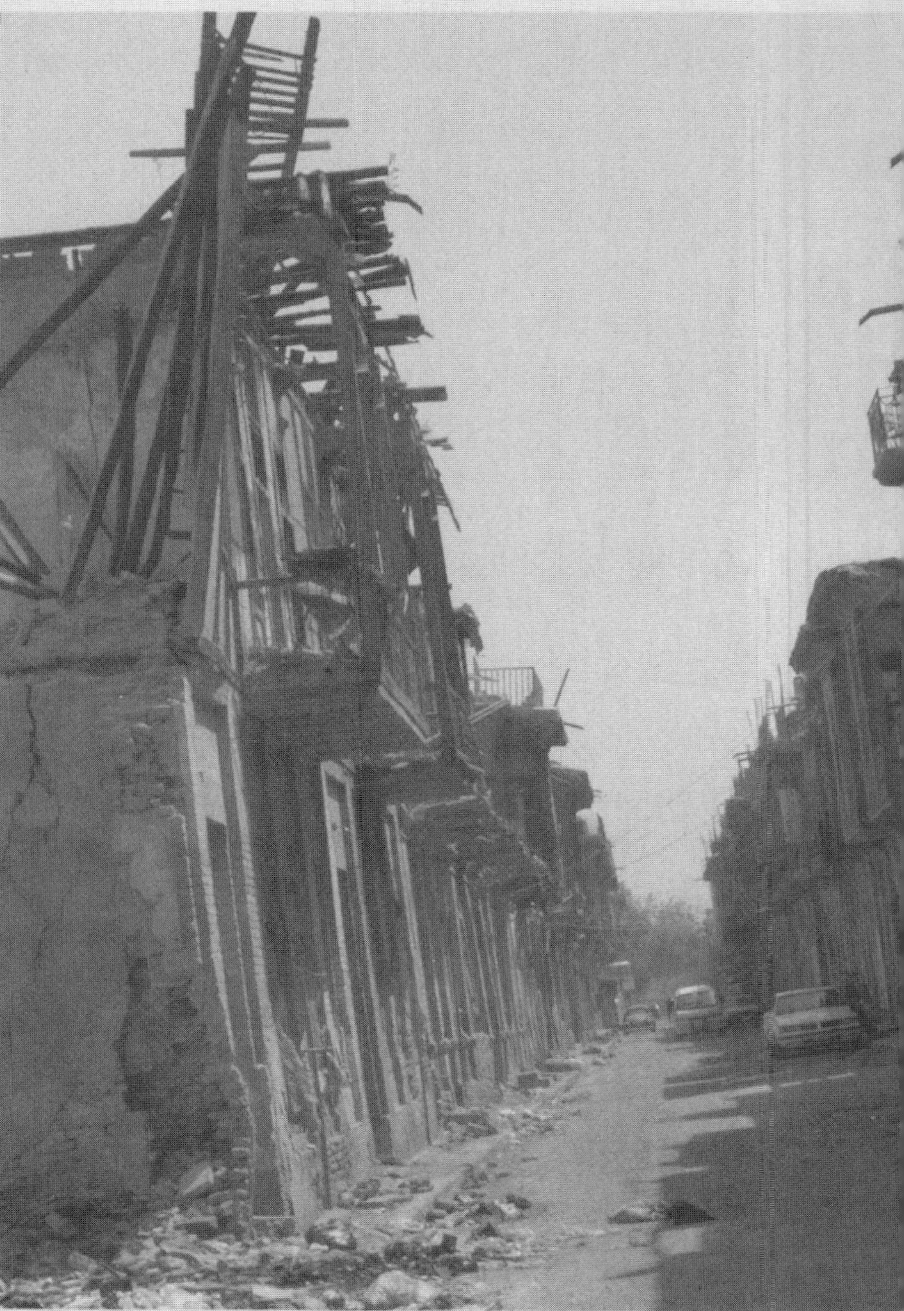

INSTANT RUINS

Once one of the most elegant areas of , th is now one of the

RETREAT

Blocking out the perils that haunt the city, an oldier from the right, takes time off at his bunker checkpoint for

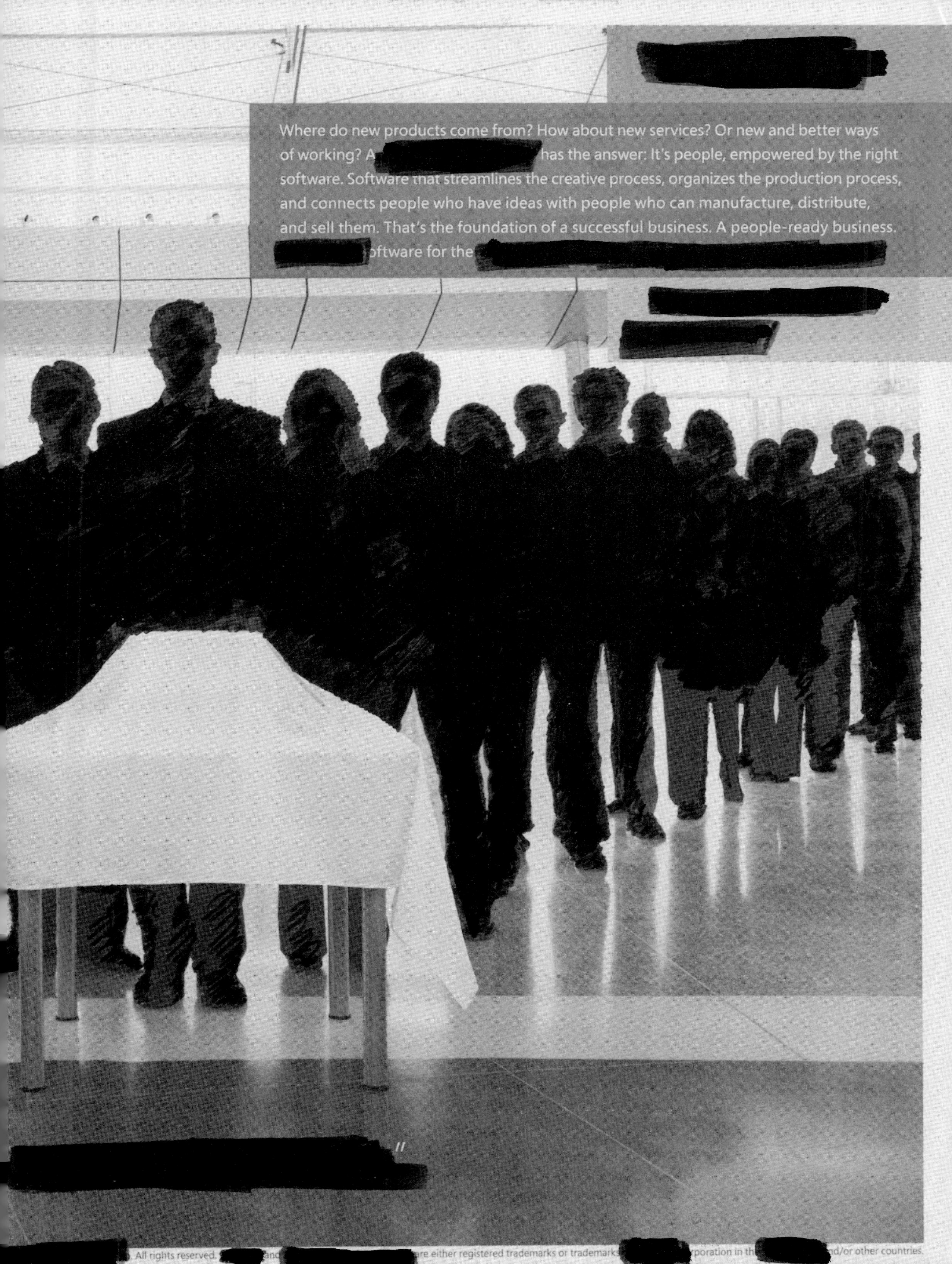
Where do new products come from? How about new services? Or new and better ways of working? A has the answer: It's people, empowered by the right software. Software that streamlines the creative process, organizes the production process, and connects people who have ideas with people who can manufacture, distribute, and sell them. That's the foundation of a successful business. A people-ready business.
oftware for the
All rights reserved. and are either registered trademarks or trademarks rporation in th nd/or other countries.

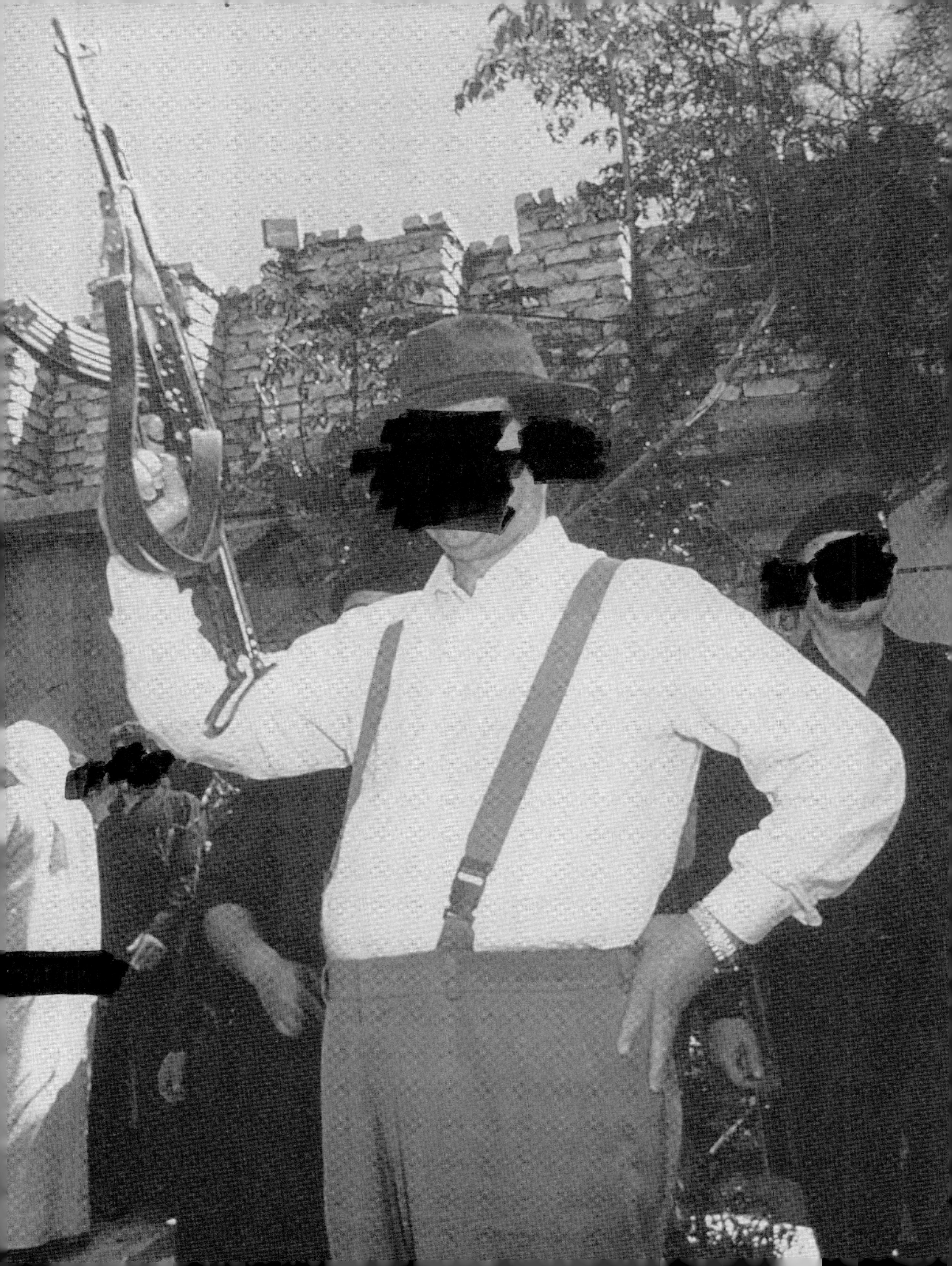

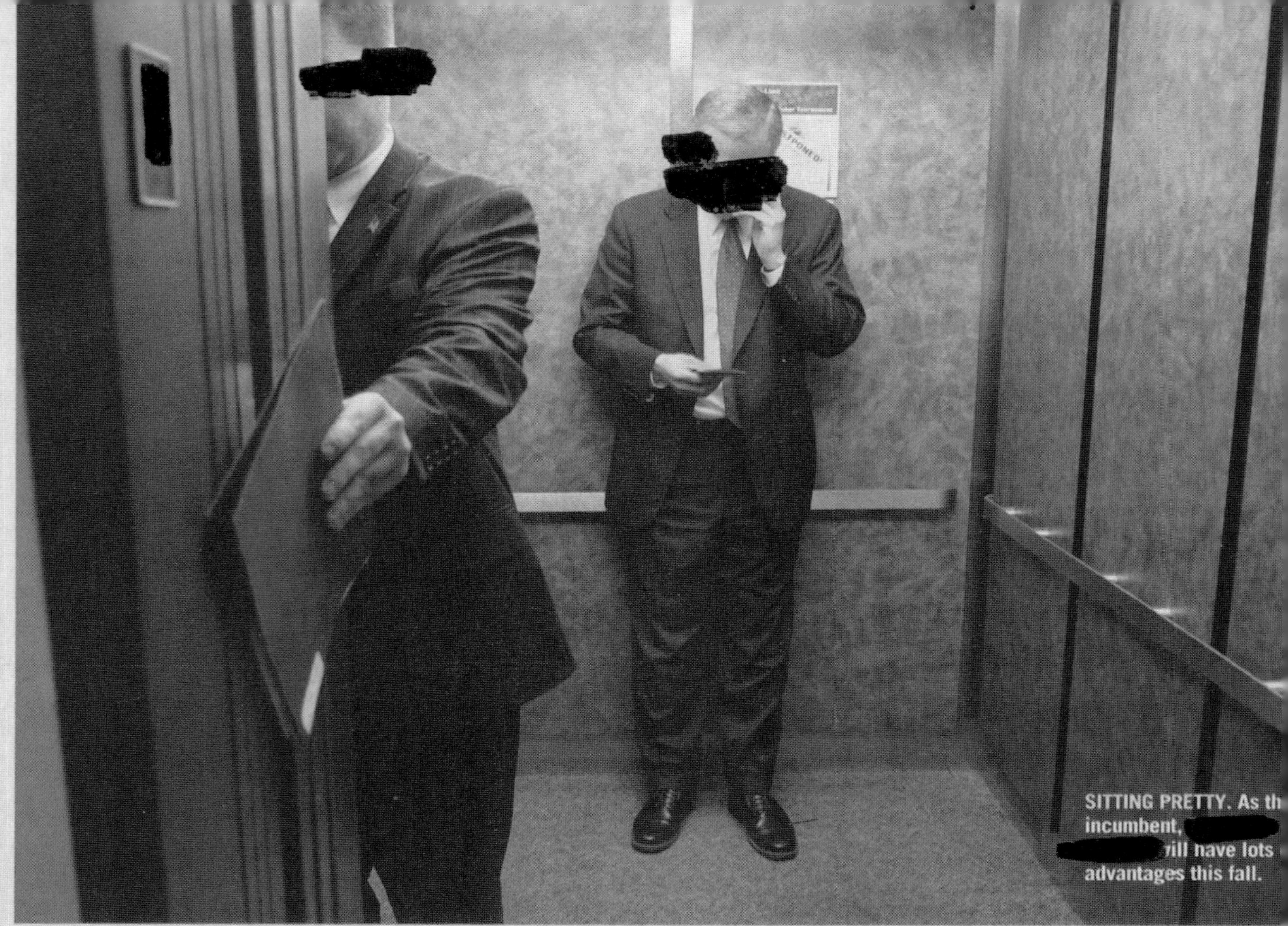

SITTING PRETTY. As th incumbent, ill have lots advantages this fall.

A FAKE DEMOCRACY?

Why no one has much chance of toppling incumbents

By

M —With the war in $3-a-gallon gas, and J dogging might seem a good bet for an ambitious lik to give up a six-figure salary and campaign for a seat in the After all, he was a top executive at started his own technology company, and makes a convincing case for bringing the lessons he's learned from business to bear on government. But was hardly the first choice to run in which fans out east and west from southern He has close to zero name recognition, entered the race late—in ary—and has no political experience. "Don't you usually start in ?" a reporter with *press* recently asked. Despite his business credentials, political analysts say, as little chance of winning.

Next week will face off with primary opponent a risk-control engineer and whose campaign faces an even steeper climb. His only big donor is his father, who gave "I refuse to ask people for money," he says, "because they'll expect something in return." Instead, is spending Saturday afternoons knocking on doors. "He seems like a friendly guy," says ear-old mother of three, after meeting him in her driveway. A publican who backed in sounds ready to support a this fall. "Spending is out of control and on the wrong things," she says. "I'm open to change."

Special Report

It's the kind of sentiment that and hundreds of candidates nationwide are seizing on in their quest to wrest control of the this . Like most of the challengers, though, whoever wins next week ere must face what has become a nearly insurmountable obstacle: an incumbent, a fact of modern political life that is making it all but impossible to change the balance of has represented since His ties to may be a

Photography by

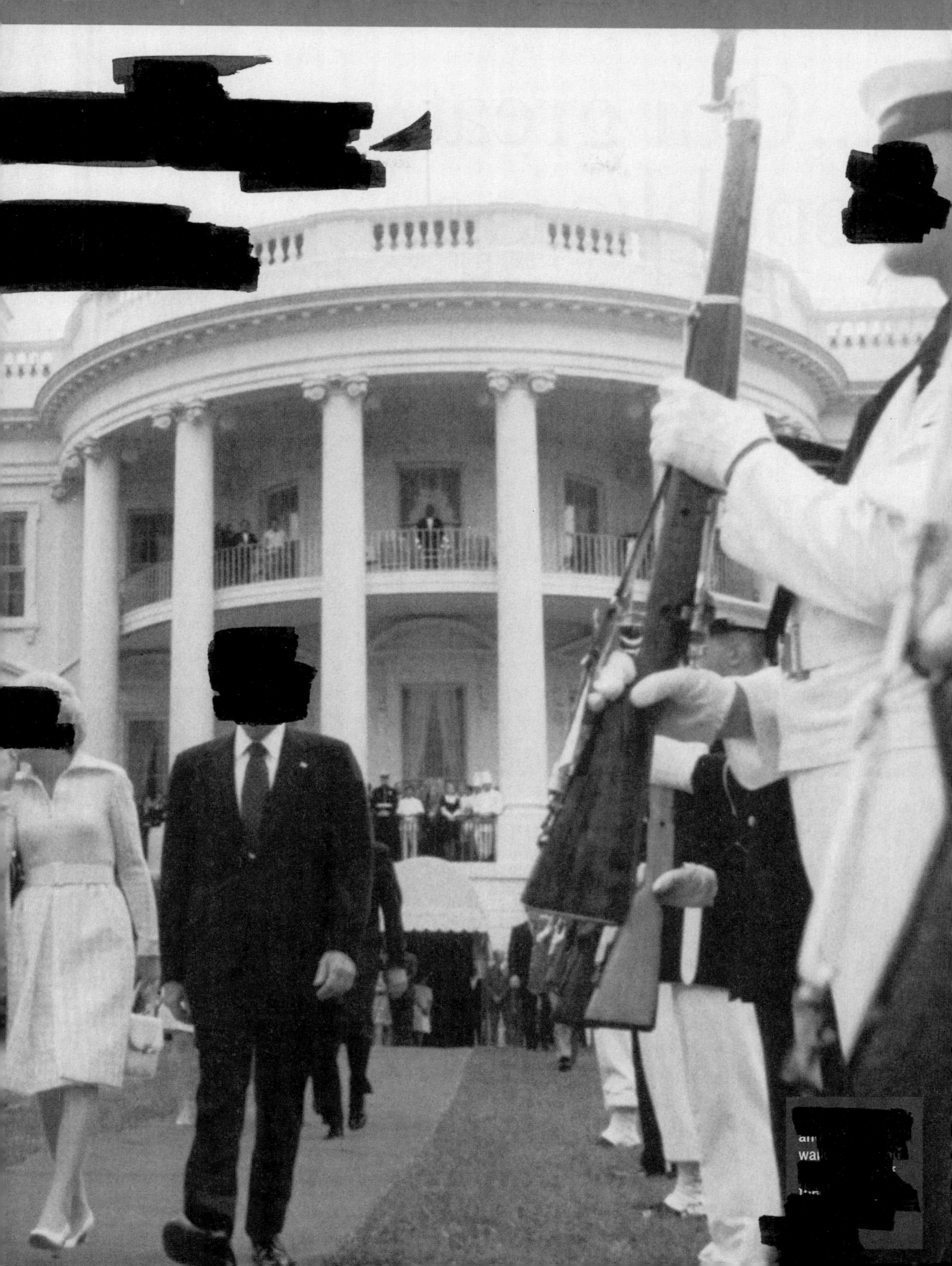

the loudest

sound ever he

will happen again.

HOW HISTORY REPEATS ITSELF

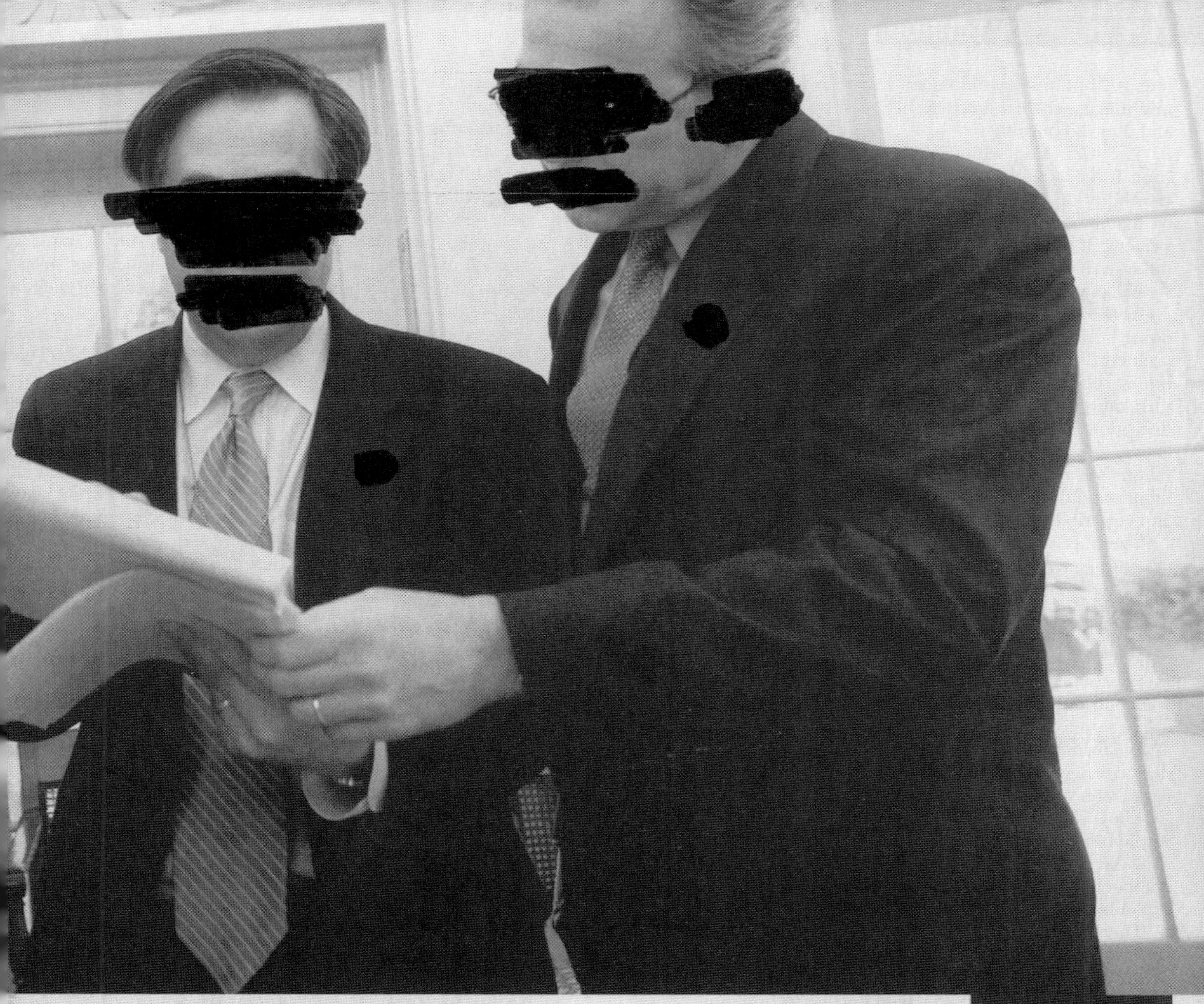

On this theory, et out a series of policy changes from the weeks afte o his secon in . Threats would be confronted before they arrive, the sponsors of terror would be held equally accountable for terrorist murders and would promot as an alternative to , the exploitation of religion to impose a violent political utopia. Every element of the doctrine was directed toward a vision: a reformed that joins the world instead of resenting and assaulting it.

That vision has been tested on nearly every front, by rockets in , car bombs in and a crackdown on dissent in calls this the "birth pangs" of a new t, and it is a complicated birth. As this violent global conflict proceeds, and its length and costs become more obvious, should keep a few things in mind.

First, the nation may be tired, but history doesn't care. It is not fair that the challenge o is rising wit bloody and unresolved. But, as used to say, "I

Behind all the chaos and death in and northern is the main cause of worry in the —the crisis with the highest stakes. Its government shows every sign of grand regional ambitions, pulling together an alliance composed of terrorist groups lik n and and proxies in and . And despite other disagreements, all the factions in —conservative, ultraconservative and "let's usher in the apocalypse" fanatics—seem united in a nuclear nationalism.

FINE PRINT: (center), anc vork on the

Some commentators say that is too exhausted to confront this threat. But decisions on national security are not primarily made by the divination of public sentiments; they are made by the determination of national interests. And the low blood-sugar level of pundits counts not at all. Here the choice is not easy, but it is simple: can (and other nations) accept a nuclea

In foreign-policy circles, it is sometimes claimed that past nuclear proliferation—say, to —has been less destabilizing than predicted. In the case of this is wishful thinking. A nuclear would mean a nuclear , as traditional rivals like , and feel pressured to join the club, giving every regional conflict nuclear overtones. A nuclear would also give terrorist groups something they have previously lacked and desperately want: a great-power sponsor. Over time, this is the surest way to put catastrophic technology into the hands of a murderous

Nor has there been much progress on other security matters. The government's claims that several insurgent groups have responded to offers of amnesty have yet to be proved; some leaders say those who have opened negotiations are fringe figures with little sway over the insurgency. As for the they seem unhindered by The market explosion proved that the lull following death was temporary. Suicide bombings have again become a daily headline. Many fit into a deadly new pattern: as crowds are drawn to the scene of the first explosion, a second device is detonated, doubling the toll. There was even a double bombing 100 yards from the main entrance of the the highly fortified enclave that houses the seat of the overnment and the headquarters of the The twin blasts—one a car bomb, the other a suicide bomber—killed people near some small shops where journalists emerging from the on hot afternoons stop to buy cold sodas. Although the is one of the most protected places in the entrance known as s one of the most dangerous. Last summe nd several othe staff members were fortunate to be just out of harm's way when a suicide bomber struck a kebab stand near the shops. The blast took the bomber's head clear off his body and sent it rolling down the road to feet. He kicked it away dismissively.

Powerless to stop the killing, government has also failed to improve the lot of the living. Crime continues to soar, especially the booming business of kidnapping for ransom officials say as many as are kidnapped every day. Ransom demands range from thousands of dollars to millions; many victims are never heard from again. Services are a cruel joke. As summer temperatures climb to 120°, there has been no perceptible improvement in electricity or the water supply. And at a time when people desperately need their gasoline-powered generators to operate ceiling fans and air conditioners, fuel has become scarce. The wait in a gas-station line can last all day. Last month the black-market rate for a liter of gas briefly reached $1—exactly 100 times the official price just before the war. My colleagues are amused when I read them stories about complaining of high gas prices.

High fuel prices have yielded one bonus: with more and more people keeping their cars at home, the roads are relatively free of traffic snarl-ups. It's typical o hat when something seems to get better—whether traffic or the ride from the airport—it's usually because something else has got much worse.

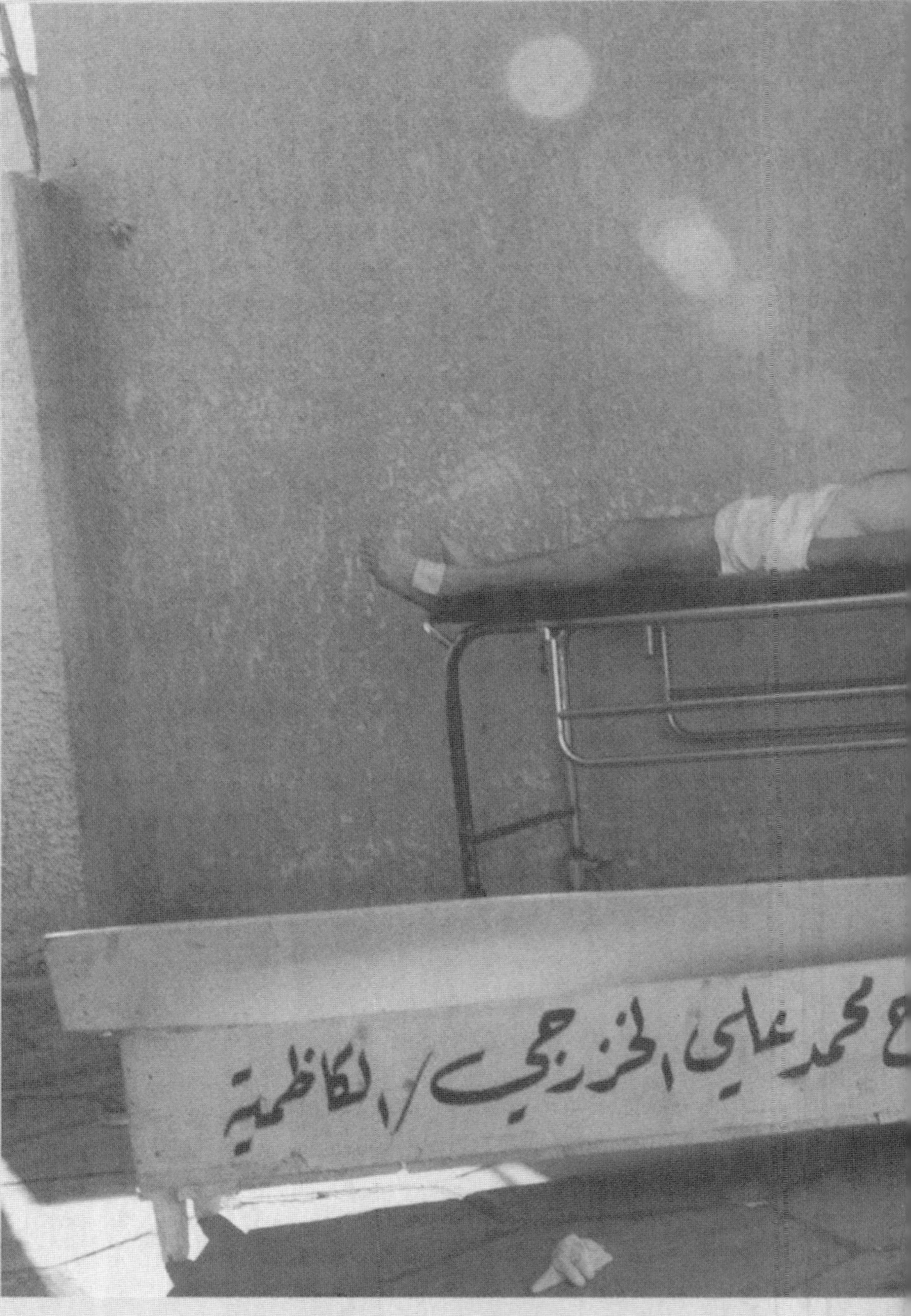

Increasingly, the attacks are taking place in leaving o wonder how can overlook large numbers of

AMID THIS UNREMITTING MISERY, STRUGGLE for some semblance of normality. In , the curfew means that the traditional family outings of summer—an evening picnic on the banks of the dinner at a kebab restaurant or a late-night drive to an ice cream parlor—are all out of the question. Visiting with friends and family is impossible unless you're prepared to go early and stay overnight. It's an especially frustrating time for children; although it's the summer break, parents are reluctant to let kids out of the house. Danger hides everywhere. Last week were among eople killed and urt when two bombs went off at a soccer field in the district of

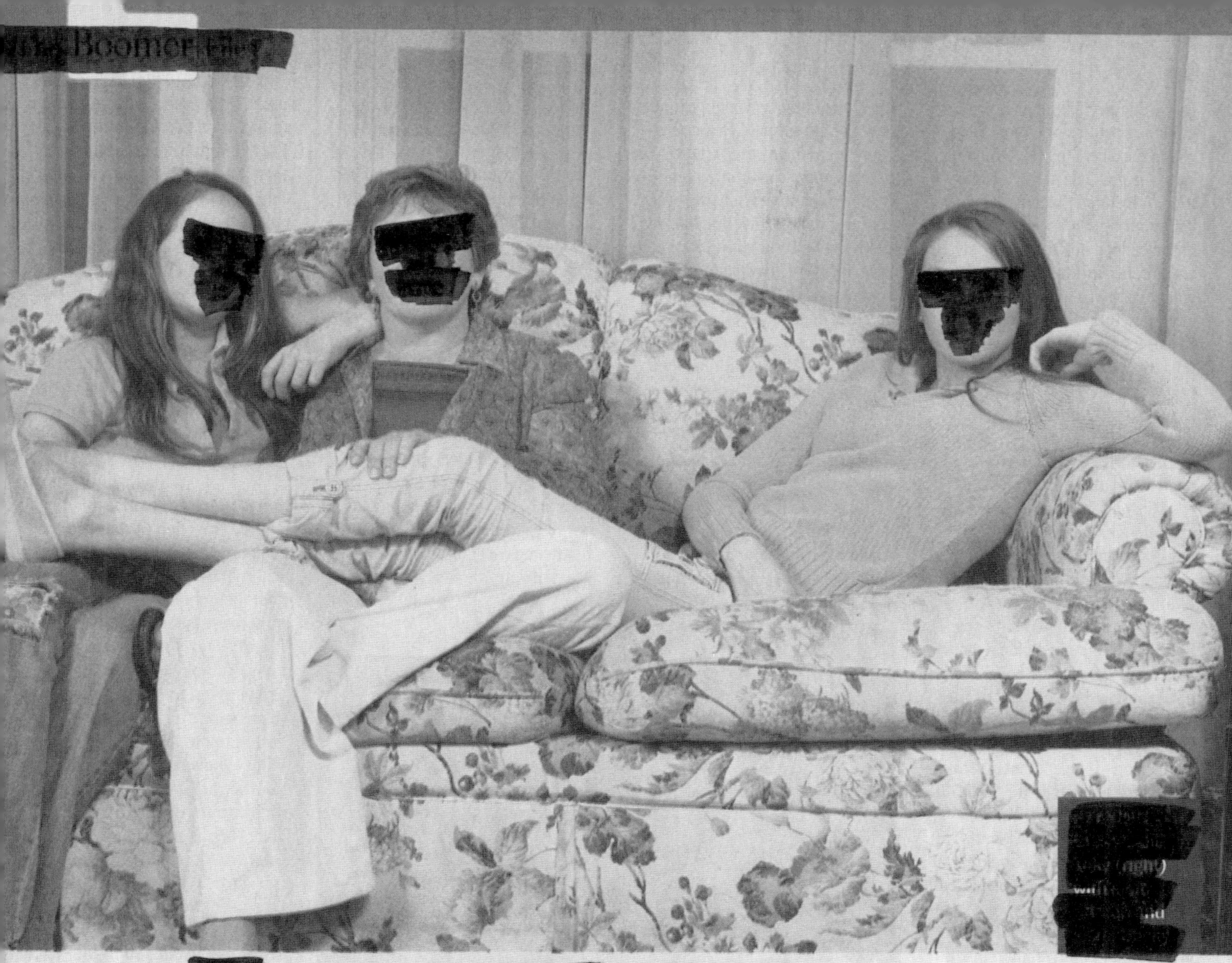

(Continued from pag

younger entered with strong reasons to find a better way to

sales manager for a beef company, was the younges ds. mother died when he was was working all the time. "There was in my house when I was who lives in was the youngest of everything is completely different from the way tha " says "My nd I dedicate our lives ." Th are now ag " says In many ways, he says he because he

some " says His daughte who' in ys the open relationship has with her keeps her out of trouble. "Because my " she says, "I don't have . We They have, for example, talked about where there might be some knows that if she did decide to all she would have to do is and someone would "Because we talk about things so much, I don't even want to she says. "It's the whose don't talk to them who sneak around and do dumb things." Her are her "That's the kind of I want to have with my in the future," she says.

But to get to that place of mutual trust and respect, do have to let go a little. "It is good and healthy for to want thei to be successful, but there are many ways to get there," says "Part of good is facilitating your not just nd her husband, are both who live in They chose their house because it is just a mile from the hospital where they work and they could be home for dinner with their and

As their grew older, and

81% of people say that,

74% of people say you must be able to

55% of people say you have to

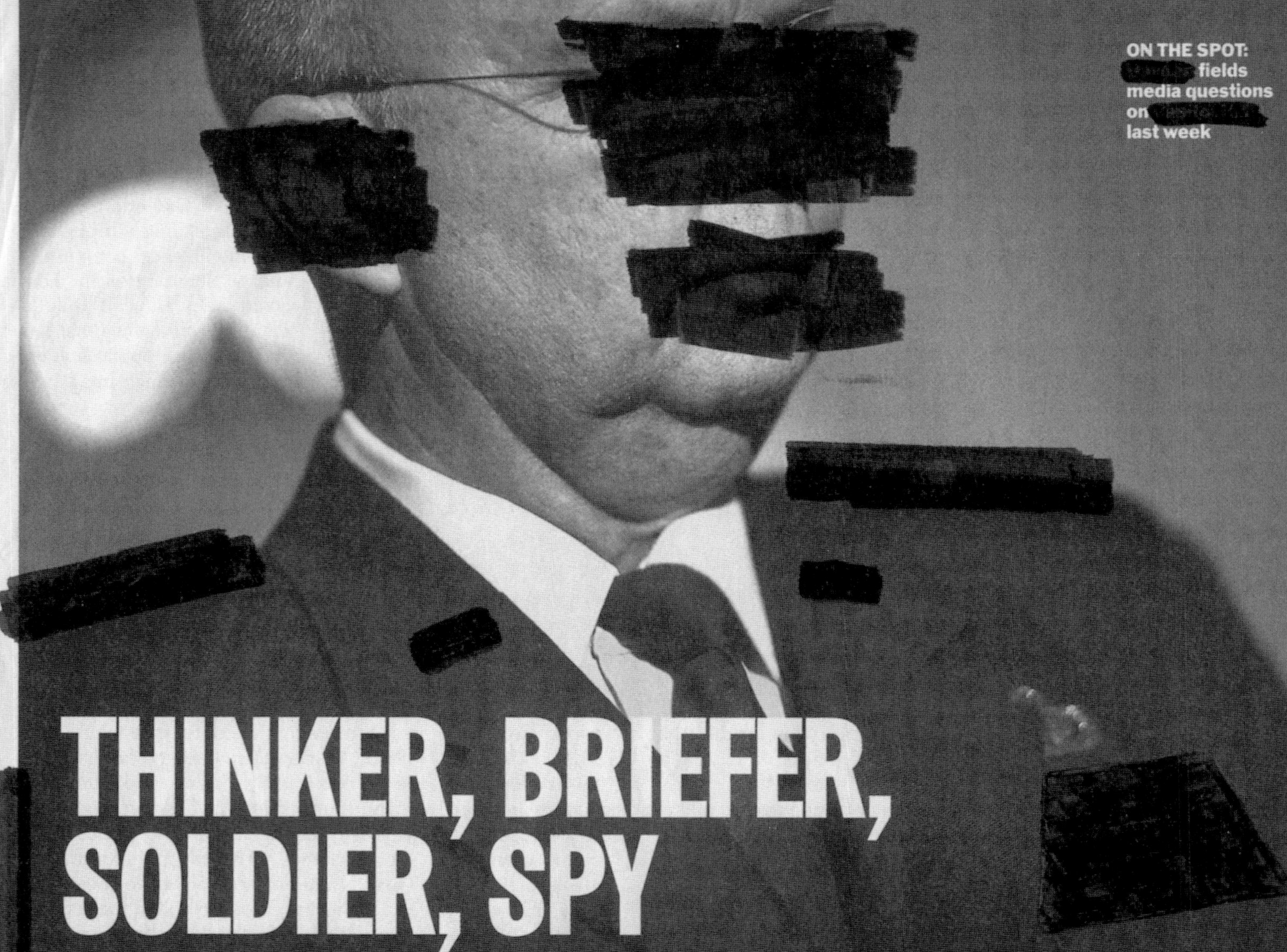

ON THE SPOT: … fields media questions on … last week

THINKER, BRIEFER, SOLDIER, SPY

Should a military man head the …? … critics say no, but … is nobody's puppet

By …

A WELDER'S JOB IS TO PUT THINGS together—hard, metal things that have to be melted and manipulated in order to be fused into something useful, like a pipeline, or a bridge. So maybe it was from his father, a welder in …, that … long ago acquired the tools that made him one of the pre-eminent intelligence players in … His great talent is the briefing, when he sits down in secret sessions with leaders in … who don't always know much about intelligence analysis, and he shows how the pieces fit together, explains how things work, lays the pipe, builds the bridge.

"…," observes former … who was chairman of the … until … "And then he pauses as if to give the listener a chance to assimilate what he has just said." It is clear when … goes to … that he has studied his audience carefully. "… says a … who has seen the general in action with lawmakers. "…" In fact, he was credited with so effectively defending the … no-warrant wiretapping program after it was exposed in … that he helped turn a simmering scandal into a political win for the … —to a degree that … might have hoped for another assist when he nominated … to replace … ," says a former … official who knows him. "…"

… is the rare officer who managed to earn four stars in the course of a career in military intelligence. A blue-collar kid who drove a taxi to help pay his way through college before joining the … his first job in … was as an analyst and briefer at the … in … He worked in intelligence in … during the … war and in … and at the … with … during the first … As … director, he sometimes dropped in on … station

> **TWO DAYS AFTER … HE TOLD HIS STRICKEN STAFF AT THE … "RIGHT NOW, A QUARTER OF A BILLION AMERICANS WISH THEY HAD YOUR JOB, TO GO AFTER THE ENEMY."**

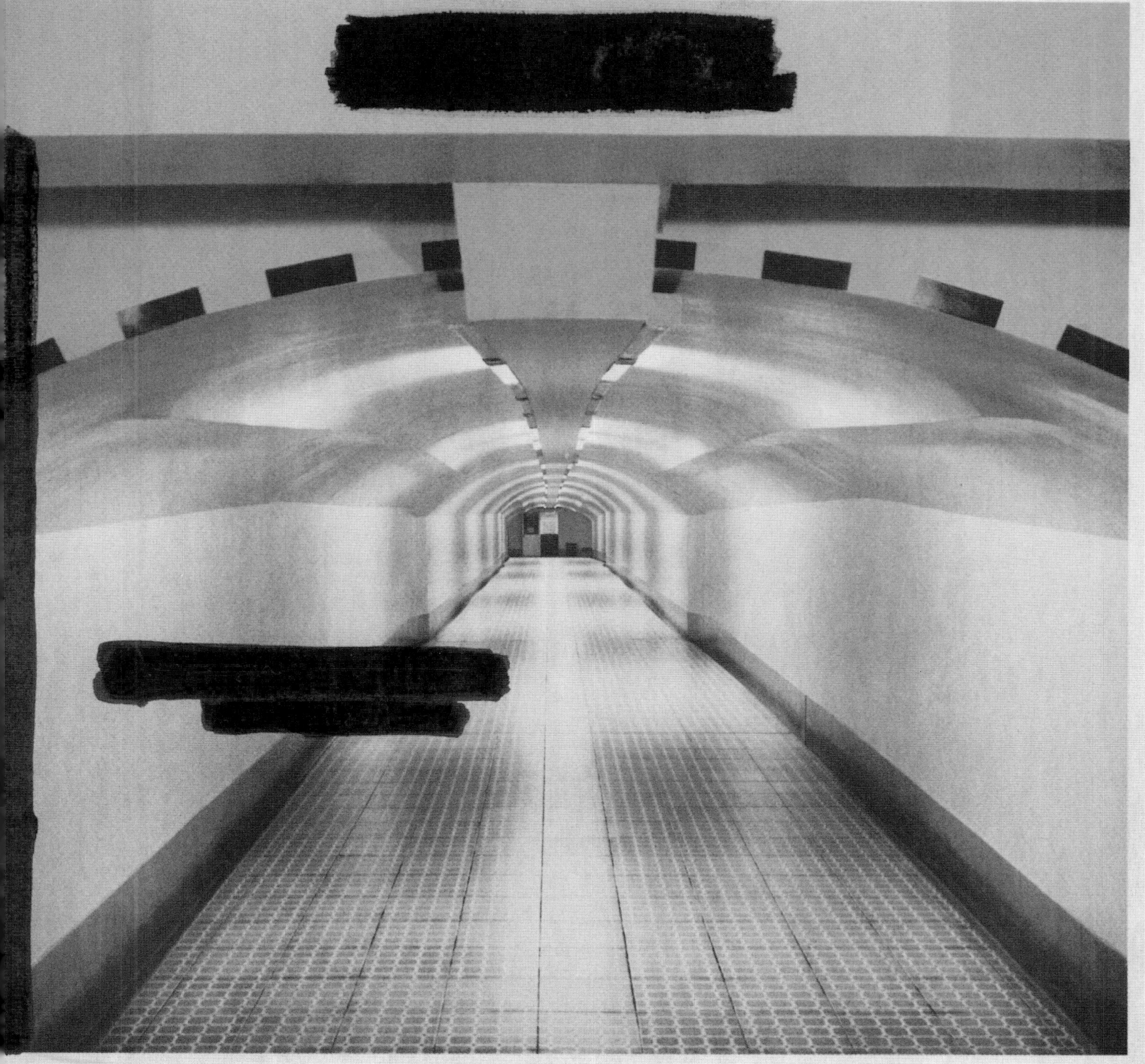

What it means to b[redacted]t means seeing the world as interconnected and flowing, and knowing how these borderless economies affect the investment decisions you make. It means having the wherewithal to invest as confidently [redacted] as in [redacted] At [redacted] an understanding of the world as more complex and more dyna[redacted]ic than it has ever been. Which means that success is not only a matter of what you've invested in, but more importantly, whom you've invested with.

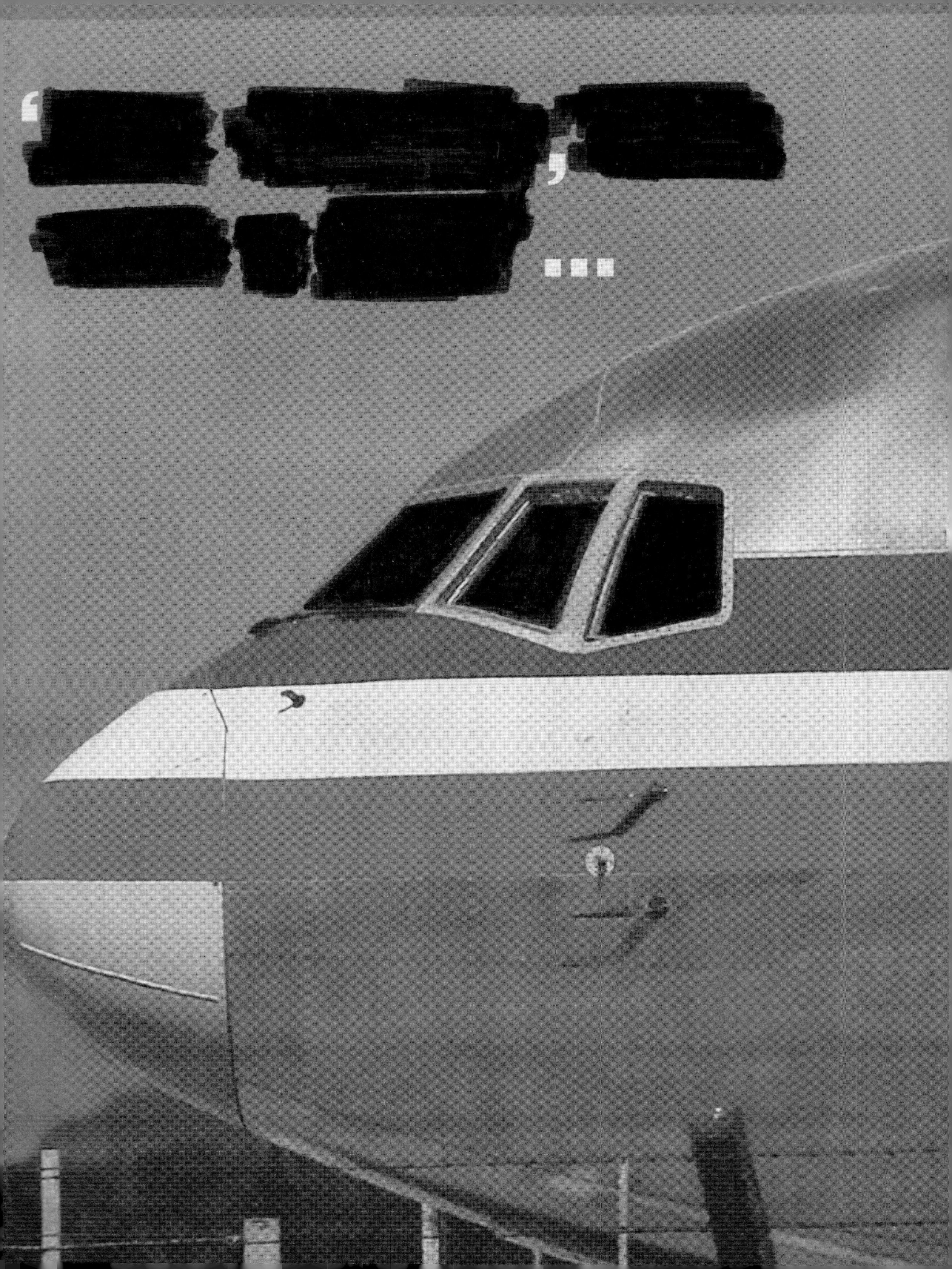